RADICAL HUMANISM

Jean Améry

RADICAL HUMANISM

Selected Essays

Edited and Translated by
Sidney Rosenfeld and Stella P. Rosenfeld

Indiana University Press

BLOOMINGTON

Manufactured in the United States of America

Library of Congress Cataloging in Publication Data

Améry, Jean.
  Radical humanism.

  Essays translated from various sources.
    1. Holocaust survivors—Germany—Addresses, essays,
lectures.   2. Antisemitism—Addresses, essays, lectures.
3. National socialism—Addresses, essays, lectures.
4. Philosophy, Modern—Addresses, essays, lectures.
I. Rosenfeld, Sidney.   II. Rosenfeld, Stella P.
III. Title.
D810.J4A623213   1984   940.53'15'03924043   83-49525
ISBN 0-253-34770-X

1 2 3 4 5 88 87 86 85 84

Contents

PREFACE
Jean Améry: The Passion of Enlightenment

In 1977, on the occasion of his sixty-fifth birthday and a year before he took his life, Jean Améry said the following of himself: "With serious doubts, I try to practice a radical humanism that now as before I would like to place on the left—despite the rather painful fact that those who regard themselves these days as leftists are about to give me up for lost, while the Right sees this as no reason to grant me its trust (something I would find dubious and firmly reject anyhow)." "Radical humanism" characterizes Améry's entire work, including the essays selected and translated for this volume. It communicates itself to the reader as the sum of those qualities that founded and upheld his position in German letters as a political and cultural essayist-critic of rare stamp and stature. Radical humanism found its expression in his loyalty to reason and enlightenment, his intellectual and personal integrity, his moral rigorism, his unwavering defense of humane values.

These qualities were strikingly evident from the start, when Améry, a survivor of SS torture and the Nazi death camps, surmounted his unwillingness to write for a German audience and in 1966 gained widespread esteem through his autobiographical essayistic study of the Auschwitz victim, *Jenseits von Schuld und Sühne*. In 1980 the English translation, *At the Mind's Limits*, introduced him in America also, where critics praised the work as a singular contribution to the literature of the Holocaust, as "the autobiography of an extraordinarily acute conscience," bearing "in every word and thought the stamp of the authentic." In America, as earlier in Germany, this book placed Améry in the forefront of those writers who, through literary confrontation with their ordeals as victims of barbarity, have given us insight, beyond the sheer physical horrors, into the essence of what must ultimately remain indescribable and inexplicable: the insane world of Nazi totalitarianism.

Améry had withstood the inferno of Auschwitz without the support of religious belief or a political ideology. He made no personal claims for his ability to survive, nor did he find in his survival any redemptive meaning. In the concentration camps, he wrote in the title chapter of *At the Mind's Limits*, "we did not become better, more human, more humane, and more mature ethically." Nor did he leave the death camp "wiser and deeper," but he could say that he was "smarter," that is, better equipped to recognize that the severest demands placed on us by reality are of a physical and social nature.

His *resentments* as a survivor, incisively examined in a further chapter of his book, emerged only later, when the natural eroding powers of time had helped to blur the singular and irreducible character of Nazism and, while the victims were still haunted by their nightmares, to restore the victimizers to respectability. To this "objective" course of events Améry opposed the radically humane demand for a "revolt against reality, which is rational only as long as it is moral" (a thought central also to his essay in the present volume, "The Time of Rehabilitation"). Holding fast to his resentments, he not only rejected a forgiving and forgetting induced by social pressure but voiced the demand, which he said was both "humane and absurd," that time itself be annulled through a moral turning-back of the clock. This subjective process would face the criminals, who were being absolved by the passage of time, with the immorality of their deeds and thus redress the moral and historical injustice, which the victims continue to bear as their personal suffering.

Améry knew that his protest against the objectification of historical events—"What happened, happened!"—would go unheeded, and his resentments found no possibility for catharsis. He witnessed, not only in the new Germany, the progressive strengthening of restorative forces and historical revisionism and with it the insidious stigmatization of the Nazi victims as the real incorrigibles of their time. The resignation and, what is most poignant, the indifference to which he gradually succumbed—a state that, along with his ruined health, led to his suicide—must be seen in direct relationship to the radicalism of his moral rebellion. At stake for him was recovery of his *trust in the world*, which had been shattered when he was compelled as a victim of torture to recognize that the social contract protecting the weak could be breached with impunity; at stake was release from the *loneliness* into which he had been plunged by the Nazis while the world stood silent.

Améry's identification with the Left is documented in the essay "Wasted Words," where he even expressed a sense of personal culpability for the failures of the Left in postwar Germany—although he had avoided that country altogether until 1964 and it was not until 1966 that his involvement there as a writer-intellectual became more pronounced. At no time, however, was he the adherent of a political doctrine or party, neither during the war, when he was active in a small communist-led group within the Belgian underground, nor in the postwar period. Of Marxism itself he said, in *At the Mind's Limits*, that it was "an ideology whose errors and false conclusions" he had already seen through long ago. Later, he declared that he had come to see in Marx "less the dialectician and successor to Hegel than the prophet of a *new morality*, the direct descendant of the very same bourgeois enlightenment that in the eyes of modern Marxists—who disregard the human being—is but an unwieldy instrument of the ruling classes" ("Enlightenment as Philosophia Perennis"). In keeping with this conviction he called for a revision of the concept of "left," from "an attitude toward the problem of economic hegemony" to "essentially a radical humanism" ("Wasted Words"). He saw the future of the Left, indeed its very existence, endangered by two developments of the late 1960s: the trend of the Left, specifically the New Left, to ally itself with fringe groups that were prone to violence, and its fixation on dialectics and social theory as absolutes. His worst fears were realized when, in the 1970s, proliferating leftist violence escalated internationally to naked terrorism.

The severest test of Améry's self-perception as a leftist intellectual came in the wake of the Arab-Israeli war of June 1967. The Left's abandonment of Israel, its support for the forces that were threatening the Jewish state with destruction, the emergence of a new antisemitism under the mantle of anti-Zionism filled him with anguish. The Auschwitz survivor, burdened with "the necessity and impossibility of being a Jew," as he had formulated it in *At the Mind's Limits*, became once again "a vehemently protesting Jew." In a newspaper commentary of June 9, 1967, entitled "Between Vietnam and Israel," he declared himself unequivocally: "Since enemy armies have been gathering about Israel, since the most unbridled voices from the Arab countries have already begun proclaiming that this small land will have to be turned into one big concentration camp, since there is talk of throwing Israel into the sea—[I am] no longer a leftist intellectual, but only a Jew." This commentary and the Brotherhood Week address translated here under the title "Antisemitism on the Left" are but two of several articles and essays of this period that witness Améry's passionate defense of Israel—and the assertion of his own authenticity, which was indissolubly bound to his Jewish identity and therewith to the fate of that country. His irrevocable solidarity with the Jewish state brought him rejection by the Left, even the loss of friendships, so that in the end he was truly "homeless on the Left" (as a section heading in his essay volume of 1971, *Widersprüche*, characterized his situation).

As a Jewish leftist intellectual Améry knew that the choice "between Vietnam and Israel," had he really been faced with it, would have been no choice at all—since the will to *authenticity* had already decided for him; but he also knew that every personal stand, however compelling, is constantly challenged by social-historical actuality. In June 1977 he openly voiced his anxiety after Menachem Begin and the Likud party, whose national-theocratic tendencies he rejected, had won the Israeli election. "The existential tie of every Jew to Israel remains," he wrote, "but it may reach the point where it becomes a burden." The courage of his convictions, even when it threatened discord with those to whom he was inseparably bound by a shared fate, marked his person indelibly.

Améry himself was ever disinclined to ascribe any such merits to his own person. From the beginning he denied the significance of his biographical self and consciously restricted its presence in his work. He regarded his experiences as the manifestations of "an ordinary fate in the most extraordinary of times," and it was the currents and conflicts that made this time so extraordinary that he aimed to reflect in his writing—in a manner that would transcend what was merely individual. Although *Jenseits von Schuld und Sühne* and the two books that followed it, *Über das Altern* (On aging) and *Unmeisterliche Wanderjahre* (Lean journeyman years), were autobiographical—he called them collectively "a kind of essayistic autobiographical novel"—they offered little of the purely factual data of his life. It was only in subsequent years, through interviews and occasional pieces in anthologies, that the portrait of his intellectual existence, which alone mattered for him, was enriched by personal detail.

The first two essays in this collection, "After Five Thousand Newspaper Articles" and "Being a Jew," are autobiographical in the traditional sense. They are meant to acquaint the reader with the course of Jean Améry's late and sorely brief career and to clarify further the question of his Jewish identity, which he probed introspectively in *At the Mind's Limits*. Although his reputation among German-language readers appears to rest largely on this, his first book, and on his much-disputed defense of suicide, *Hand an sich legen* (1976), his work documents a wide range of political and literary-cultural interests. As in the previous century for another German writer-in-exile, Heinrich Heine, France had become his second cultural homeland, and he was, in fact, a respected interpreter of contemporary French, as well as German, intellectual issues. He was sought after as a participant in symposiums and public forums; he read whole series of literary essays for radio broadcast, and in 1977 began to contribute a regular "film diary" to the journal *Merkur*. In addition to the five major works already cited, he also published two novels, *Lefeu oder Der Abbruch* (1974; Lefeu or the demolition) and *Charles Bovary, Landarzt* (1978; Charles Bovary, country doctor). Three essay volumes appeared posthumously: the autobiographical *Örtlichkeiten* (1980; Places and stations), a collection of literary criticism, *Bücher aus der Jugend unseres Jahrhunderts* (1981; Books from the young days of our century), and the mainly political-philosophical collection *Weiterleben—aber wie?* (1982; Carry on—but how?). On the side, as it were, he wrote copiously for newspapers, journals, and topical anthologies.

Above all, our selection is meant to illustrate both the diversity of Améry's literary-intellectual interests and the moral fervor with which he pursued them. Beside the expressly autobiographical essays that introduce the collection, others, too, help to bring his individuality and the evolvement of his thought into clearer focus. Almost all the essays are intensely personal, that is, informed by "the emotion that befits a good cause," as he himself put it in his address on antisemitism and the Left. Emotion is present as the confident, righteous anger of the survivor and witness in the essay on "The

Time of Rehabilitation"; it is present in the homage to Sartre as critical reverence for the philosopher whose existentialism had uplifted Améry in his quest for self-realization after the degradations of Auschwitz, and as the sorrow he felt at Sartre's fall from greatness; emotion pervades Améry's scornful rejection of Simone Weil, whose religious mysticism and neo-irrationalism the enlightener and defender of reason could neither comprehend nor tolerate. Not seldom in Améry's writing, as in his essay on the Warsaw Ghetto, this "emotion that befits a good cause" ascends to a pathos that is not declamatory or otherwise affected, but rather legitimized and authenticated by the integrity of his example as man and writer.

The twelve essays translated in this volume were written between the years 1967 and 1978. We selected them from a number of sources, mainly from the literary and political-cultural journals to which Jean Améry regularly contributed. Some were first delivered as radio talks or formal addresses and later published in anthologies; some appeared posthumously (for bibliographical data, see the source notes at the beginning of each chapter.) In all but one instance, that of "Antisemitism on the Left," we have translated the titles of the essays more or less literally. In three instances, "After Five Thousand Newspaper Articles," "In the Waiting Room of Death" and "Wasted Words," we have added a descriptive subtitle. Translations from works quoted by Améry are our own.

We wish to thank Inter Nationes (Bonn) for support in making this translation possible. We are indebted also to Dr. Hubert Arbogast and Frau Edda Both of Klett-Cotta Publishers (Stuttgart) for their valuable assistance. To Mme Maria Améry (Brussels), we express deep gratitude for her help and encouragement. Her warm friendship has inspired our efforts.

Sidney Rosenfeld
Stella P. Rosenfeld

RADICAL HUMANISM

After Five Thousand Newspaper Articles
How I Became a Writer

IT IS A WIDELY KNOWN, almost trivial fact that every piece of writing, even a theoretical one, has an autobiographical background, an autobiographical substratum. It is just a matter of the degree and density of the autobiographical element that finds its way into the work. To speak of my own case is somewhat difficult for me, since I must mention far too much that is quite personal and could easily be misunderstood as an anecdotal extra. The autobiographical component of the present piece is especially great; more precisely: I have to report on a personal and intellectual life that became a contemplative essay. By this I mean three closely related books that together embrace four decades of my intellectual life and that, in response to the editor's inquiry, I would probably have to designate as "my first major literary work." They are *Jenseits von Schuld und Sühne*, *Über das Altern*, and *Unmeisterliche Wanderjahre*.[1]

What most likely differentiates these books, as concerns their genesis, from most of the works cited in this series is the rather unusual and for me somewhat melancholy fact that they were published

"Nach fünftausend Zeitungsartikeln," in *Wie ich anfing . . . 24 Autoren berichten von ihren Anfängen* (How I began . . . 24 authors tell of their beginnings), ed. Hans Daiber (Düsseldorf: Claassen, 1979), pp. 215–26. This essay was originally read by Améry on the radio.

very late in my life. When I began writing *Jenseits von Schuld und Sühne*, I was fifty-two years old. When the third volume of the autobiography, *Unmeisterliche Wanderjahre*, appeared, I found myself in the paradoxical position of being a "promising beginner" of fifty-eight. Such a special case deserves and demands thorough illumination. Permit me, then, to begin by reproducing here in catchwords the biographical sketch that I usually send to my publishers or to interested editors when they ask for one. Jean Améry, born in 1912 in Vienna. Studied philosophy and literature there. After the annexation of Austria in 1938, emigration to Belgium. During the war participation in the Belgian resistance movement. Arrest by the Gestapo in 1943 and deportation to various German concentration camps, among them Auschwitz, Buchenwald, Bergen-Belsen. Since liberation in 1945, freelance writer and journalist.

According to these particulars, then, my literary career should have begun at least twenty-seven years ago. One could well expect more than three slim volumes that I can designate, not without irony, as "a major literary work." Did I idle away my time during those twenty-seven years or, to vary Rilke, did I write only when I would have died if I had been unable to write? No, unfortunately. If I attempt to estimate the quantity of what I committed to paper during this period, then I arrive at the dismaying figure of some five thousand newspaper articles that together would amount to about 15,000 pages, an almost frighteningly voluminous production. Of these 15,000 pages only the circa 450 of the above-mentioned autobiographical trilogy appear to me to be at all worth mentioning. This is a circumstance that I alluded to in *Jenseits von Schuld und Sühne* and in *Unmeisterliche Wanderjahre*. But it must be impressed on my audience once more—to be sure, briefly and clearly—if this text is to have any informational value at all.

As an emigrant who had been affected by the Nuremberg racial laws, as a resistance fighter and former Auschwitz inmate, for years I had found it mentally and morally impossible to work in, or for, Germany. Not until a generation of young intellectuals, newspaper and radio editors, publishers' readers, and critics had arisen who were no longer associated in my mind with the Germany of the deepest humiliation—mine and the country's own—not until I could again meet Germans impartially, did I feel free to work for German media. This was not possible before 1964, when I had a chance meeting in Brussels with Helmut Heissenbüttel, in whose person I encountered for the first time since 1933 a new and truly "other" Germany. Until this point I was compelled to earn my living as a journalist in the relatively tiny German-language market of Alemannic Switzerland; and there an unshakable law of the marketplace determined my path. While I was no longer young, I was totally unknown. As much as I wanted, I could have never found the means that would have enabled me to devote myself to a major work. There was no demand for the philosophic-sociological essays I was offering, let alone for books of this kind. Since I went on writing in the German language and managed just about halfway correct but stylistically flat texts in French, for nearly two decades I produced feuilletonistic and sometimes also political articles for Swiss daily and weekly papers that guaranteed me a certain external subsistence.

My identity as a writer, which I had been seeking since my sixteenth year, when my first manuscript was printed in Vienna, had vanished. I accustomed myself to the situation of a failure or a "raté," as I preferred to say in French (because it sounded less dramatic and pathetic). In any case, in my own eyes I could claim the mitigating circumstances of an ordinary fate in the most extraordinary of times and tell myself that I belonged to a truly "lost" generation and to a lost domain of language. Only when I rediscovered this domain of language in its total dimensions did I discover myself as a writer too. But it was high time. Perhaps it was already far too late. At an age when others were harvesting, I began timidly to feel my way along and sow seed.

As I have already said, it was Helmut Heissenbüttel—whom I had met by chance—whom I vaguely told of my plan to make my experiences in the underground and the concentration camp the subject of philosophical speculation—since at that time the big Auschwitz trial was being prepared in Frankfurt. He immediately offered me his "Radio Essay" department of the South German Broadcasting Corporation as a forum. I agreed without hesitation, as though everything between Germany and me had suddenly been cleared up (which naturally was also an illusion, but I realized that only when I began writing). The radio series of five essays appeared as a book in 1966. Gerhard Szczesny, cofounder of the Humanistic Union, editor of the yearbook *Club Voltaire*, writer and publisher, took up the cause. At the same time, Hans Paeschke, the editor of the monthly magazine *Merkur*, took notice of me and asked me to become a contributor to his periodical. This, then, was my entry into German literature. I was fifty-four years old when my name slowly, very slowly began to mean something to a limited sector of the German reading public.

With the book *Jenseits von Schuld und Sühne*, first published by Szczesny and reprinted by Klett-Cotta years later, I achieved what is called a *succès d'estime*, the saddest kind of success, as an English writer whose name escapes me once said, not without reason. The critics were friendly. The *Zeit* printed an appreciation from the pen of Horst Krüger, the *Spiegel* joined in with a kind of little write-up, numerous important German newspapers and radio stations followed. I am still not sure whether it was the intellectual and literary quality of the slim volume that I had to thank for its *succès d'estime* or whether it was the material treated in it: Auschwitz, the Jewish Question, torture, emigration. I have the suspicion that I merely struck a chord that began to vibrate just at a time when it was still fashionable to occupy oneself with the fate of the Nazi victims, and that today, when my friends on the Left are representing Israel as a universal plague and everyone's sympathies are focusing on the Palestinian resistance fighters, I couldn't tempt a soul with this book. Moreover, even if at that time the response by the critics was considerable, among the public it was modest enough. If I recall correctly, a mere seven thousand copies of the title (as publisher's language puts it) were sold. Not a very impressive result. But the ice was broken in any case, and more and more radio and television stations, as well as daily and weekly papers, invited me to contribute.

Perhaps at this point I may parenthetically bring up an economic problem of free-lance writing. I have the impression that aside from a few very successful or moderately successful authors, most of us free lances would be unable to exist economically without the much-maligned "media." For the independent writer, radio and television occupy the social position today that was once held by the patrons of art. I know that in saying this I am acting contrary to Heinrich Böll's demand that an end be put to modesty. And maybe one really should not offer considerations like these on the radio (of all places), so as not to make the situation of the free-lance writer even more precarious than it already is. But I am reluctant to show such consideration for my colleagues and myself. Again and again, whenever I read sometimes quite difficult and demanding texts into a radio microphone, I ask myself uneasily: Who is going to listen to this? And then the medium really does appear to me as an anonymous patron and promoter or, if one wishes to view it differently and perhaps just as validly, a supporter of cultural policies that receive no backing from the federal and state governments.

But now back to my own work. I had escaped the drudgery of writing articles in 1966. I could contemplate writing about the things that were weighing on my soul. And as a late beginner I began with the autobiographical theme. First of all, this placed the decisive personal problem, the crux of my existence, at the center: aging. Clearly, the mere fact that as a person in the middle of the sixth decade of his life I was at the point in my career as a writer where others are at thirty or thirty-five, was reason enough to find aging especially painful. I was just starting out and at the same time I was already galloping at full speed toward the end. Given such circumstances, it would not have even required a weakened state of physical health to make the problem of aging the main concern of my writing. The influences of reading contributed their share. At that time I had just read the dramatic last pages of the third volume of Simone de Beauvoir's recollections, *Force of Circumstances*, in French and the splendid essay of Sartre's pupil André Gorz, "Le vieillissement," and also—last, not least—the unusually fascinating contribution to the philosophy of corporeality by the German doctor and anthropologist Herbert Plügge (who meanwhile, alas, had died all too early). Proust's uncanny, grandiose phenomenology of aging, set down in the last volume of *Remembrance of Things Past*, had been around me and in me for years anyway. Thus equipped, I began writing my second autobiographical book, *Über das Altern*. I ask myself, to be sure, whether and to what extent the designation "autobiographical," which is debatable even in the case of *Jenseits von Schuld und Sühne*, can be legitimately applied to my book on aging. I completely omitted everything private or anecdotal. I was concerned not with stories about myself but rather with reflections on existence and the passage of time that would begin introspectively but ascend to ever more abstract and general areas of thought; reflections on the nature of being sick and on death—which I said was "nothing, a nothing, a nullity" but at the same time also the outermost reference point of all our activity and striving.

The book did not appear with Szczesny, which had ceased to exist, but was published in the fall of 1968 by Klett, the house that puts out *Merkur*. Naturally, it first had to be read for the radio so that writing it would become economically feasible. And again, it was the South German Broadcasting Corporation, or Helmut Heissenbüttel, who gave me the first chance, as they also did two years later, by the way, with the third part of the autobiography, *Unmeisterliche Wanderjahre*. Oddly enough, the new work gained just a bit more than a *succès d'estime*. In the course of three years Klett was able to issue three printings. In view of the distinct unpleasantness of the theme and the difficulty of some of my trains of thought, this amazed no one more than me. Had I once more merely caught a propitious moment? Maybe. I believe, at any rate, that it was one of the first books in postwar Germany that dealt with the problem of aging, or dealt with it in a way that did not offer cheap consolation and promise readers that their life could "begin" at fifty or sixty. I said a clear "no" to that sort of well-meant nonsense. The tragedy of aging, old age, and death was presented and analyzed phenomenologically as such, in all of its horror. As I literally wrote back then, it was an undertaking that had to end all the more "disconsolingly" since I did not seek escape in religion. I spoke as a complete atheist: death retained its terrible sting; time did not dissolve into transcendent eternity.

With very few exceptions, in which there was criticism of a "defeatist" undertaking, as someone wrote, the reception of the book was, once again, quite favorable. This time, too, *Zeit* and *Spiegel* contributed; again, almost every important German newspaper or periodical followed suit. Once more, a phenomenon similar to that after the publication of *Jenseits von Schuld und Sühne* became evident: If after the appearance of the latter book I had virtually become a "professional Auschwitz survivor," from whom people wanted to hear nothing else except commentaries on questions of Jewish identity and the existence of the victim, now I was suddenly the professional *senex*. From every likely and unlikely place people were requesting statements from me on the problem of the "third age," as though I were a gerontologist. This was an expression of the same market phenomenon, hostile to the intellect, about which so many painters lament when they are exhorted by their agents to stick by all means to their "style." The label triumphs over the law of change. My label now read "Old Age," and it cost me some effort to convince the buyers or the dealers in the intellectual consumer goods I was producing that the problems of old age were not the only subject about which I might have something to say.

I finally escaped the old-age boom. But I adhered to my autobiographical themes. I had written on two crucial experiential complexes of my existence: on my aging, which occupied me with special intensity as a result of the frighteningly late start of my literary "career" (a word that I can only write in quotation marks), and on the fate of emigration and concentration camp imprisonment, which was responsible for this late start. I had, in the broadest sense, *subjectively* explored both complexes of problems. Now I was eager for more objectivity. Without being able to depart entirely from autobiography, I wanted to reflect in it the times, *my* time. Between 1930 and 1970 I had, after all, been witness to intellectual dramas and struggles that were worth talking about. On the one hand, I had gone the road, geographically, from Austria, or Germany, to France. On the other hand, after the first unsure intellectual steps of a provincial would-be poet lost in the daydreams of irrationalism, and the uncertain gropings of a philosopher inclined toward neopositivism, I had accustomed myself to what I hope was the halfway firm gait of a liberated, contemplative person with a rather good command of existential-Marxist topography. I had experienced Austrian clerico-fascism, the outbreak of the Third Reich, the intellectual world of the Résistance, the great disenchantment after the end of the war, the development of what is today called the "consumer society." The fabulous power of fashion in all sectors of intellectual life was just as much a part of my time as the liquidation of the values that were presented to me in my youth by the older generation as "eternal" and sacred. All of that was well worth talking about. And proceeding ever anew from my personal experience, while never granting it more than minimal attention, I began writing the third part of my autobiography, the book that is dearest to me of all that I have written: the essay volume *Unmeisterliche Wanderjahre*.

This book also appeared with Klett, and that perhaps requires an explanation. After all, how does a rather pronouncedly leftist author come to be published by a house that all in all tends to be conservative? *Über das Altern* had landed at Klett more or less accidentally: Szczesny, my publisher at that time, had gone out of business and upon the recommendation of the monthly journal *Merkur* Klett agreed to put out the book quickly, by the deadline arranged with Szczesny. In the case of *Unmeisterliche Wanderjahre* the element of chance had already been eliminated. I had a choice; for although I was anything but a bestselling author, a number of big German publishing houses were interested in me. I remained with Klett because I appreciated the generous attitude of the publisher and because my consultations with the chief literary editor, Dr. Hubert Arbogast, had already taken on the character of a friendship.

The book appeared in the spring of 1971, and again the reception ranged from cordial to eulogistic. With very few exceptions, the reviews I happened to see in newspapers, weeklies, monthlies, and from the radio were such that allowed me to bank on success. But a commercial success did not materialize at all—despite the German Critics Prize, which I was awarded after the book was published (so that it was decked out with a shiny red ribbon). How come? That is what I ask myself and the publisher asks himself also. Neither he nor I will ever know. There is nothing more capricious than the external fate of a literary work. Was the text difficult? Certainly, it was even "bulky freight," as one critic wrote. I had built into it numerous literary citations that I had not designated as such; in general, I did not want to disregard the cultural tradition since it is, after all, just as much a part of my theme as it is of me. On the other hand, when I reread this work it seems to me infinitely easier to digest than the countless sociological texts that are tossed onto the market by various German publishing houses, practically in series, and apparently find their buyers (despite their involved jargon, which all too often only disguises wretched trivialities). I personally regretted the fact that once again my success had been limited to a *succès d'estime*, and the pleasure I could take in this "estime" now stood in an ever more consternating disproportion to the economic outcome. As an explanation, I can offer the following hypothesis: On the one hand, *Unmeisterliche Wanderjahre* was written by an author who makes no concessions whatever to a conservative, or culturally conservative, milieu, behind which he always senses reaction, something he detests. On the other hand, the book sometimes strikes a sharp, polemical tone in regard to fashionable intellectual trends like structuralism, for example, or certain forms of modern poetry and the visual arts. It appears to me, then, that in this way I drove off my potential conservative readership without simultaneously gaining readers who span the spectrum from progressive to radical. Especially through my criticism of the New Left I may have become a ridiculous fossil in the eyes of those readers and buyers on whom publications such as *Kursbuch*, for instance, can rely. But the Right, which has a very sure instinct, considers me to be a subversive character, someone with whom it does not want to get involved, and this view was not altered by the fact that a conservative group, the Bavarian Academy of Fine Arts, awarded me its literary prize in 1972. Need I even add that my uncomfortable position between all of the parties seems to me appropriate to my writing, even if, at the same time, I am naturally not free of a certain disappointment? You can't have your cake and eat it too. Of course, whoever says this runs the risk of winding up with no cake at all.

Precisely because this third and most certainly last part of the autobiography did not receive the response I had hoped for, I believed that I was on the right track with it. One must become independent of the size of printings and, in general, all external signs of success. Is it possible? This is a problem that extends beyond all subjectively psychological determinants into the societal realm. There is most certainly no total self-sufficiency in the case of literary creation. The poet who writes for his desk drawer is, like the poetaster-friend of the bank director John Gabriel Borkman, an absurdity, a laughingstock and a painful disgrace. But the author of a literary work who constantly steals a glance into the mirror, in the vain attempt to see himself as a society that in the end is reduced to a literary market might see him, is no less grotesque. The writer must be able to distinguish between legitimate success, which lies in the respect accorded him by like-feeling people, or, more precisely, by a certain community of like taste or mind, and purely commercial success, which is incalculable and unpredictable and scarcely has anything to do with the inherent qualities of a work.

I admit that this is not always easy, either emotionally or in the sense of a rational analysis of the facts. I myself often enough became fearsome and depressed when I had to conclude that my work was not rewarded by the epoch, a work that was written out of the epoch and for it, a work that from the start could not be expected to reach posterity (which is always a problematic concept anyhow). But when I recently read that in over a year barely ten thousand copies of Sartre's monumental work on Flaubert were sold in France, it was a certain consolation for me—although I naturally am not drawing any unseemly comparisons between myself and the greatest thinker of the present. The probability that my three books, *Jenseits von Schuld und Sühne*, *Über das Altern*, and *Unmeisterliche Wanderjahre*, and thus my existence, my life were taken note of by a few thousand people after all, and that in this way I reached other people's spheres of consciousness, is for me, to quote in a most old-fashioned way, "reward that is richly rewarding," reward that I contentedly and gratefully pocket, with a modesty that, I hope, is in no way affected.

Being a Jew
A Personal Account

AMONG MY UNFORGETTABLE memories are those of the Christian feasts, especially the midnight mass at Christmas. If I try just a bit I am also still able to recite the Catholic Creed by heart. In such circumstances, how am I supposed to, how can I, speak of "my Judaism"? It did not exist. I was nineteen years old when, in the city of my birth, Vienna—more or less cast out and exiled from the Upper Austrian province—I first learned of the existence of a Yiddish language. On the other hand, there was my mother's sister, like her a war widow, who lived with us and often gave me the soothing assurance that she would pray for me to Saint Anthony, her favorite saint; she maintained that in the most extreme distress he always helped. What had to take place so that today I not only dare to speak of "my Judaism" here, but I say at every available opportunity: I *am* a Jew?

My father was a full-blooded Jew, born in Hohenems in Vorarlberg. I didn't know him. For I was born in 1912 and in 1914 he joined the army of the Austro-Hungarian monarchy as a Tyrolean Royal Rifleman. In 1916 he was killed in the war. If I try to reconstruct his

Améry first presented this essay as a radio address in 1977. It was subsequently printed without title in the collection *Mein Judentum* (My Judaism), ed. Hans Jürgen Schulz (Stuttgart: Kreuz Verlag, 1978), pp. 78–89.

Judaism I arrive at no clear result. It seems that he hardly bothered about the religious community to which he officially belonged. His own father, my grandfather therefore, was for his part already very much estranged from his Jewish origins.

My mother's case was more complicated. She was a Christian but not "purely aryan," as I learned later. Several times a day she invoked Jesus, Mary, and Joseph, which sounded in our native dialect like "Jessasmarandjosef." She rarely went to church; just on important holidays. The prayer that she taught me was short: "Dear God, make me devout so that I can go to heaven." I muttered it mechanically to myself in the evening, maybe until my ninth year, then I dropped it. So I didn't become devout and heaven will remain closed to me. Now and then Mother used the one Jewish expression that I ever heard from her lips: *nebbich*. In our home there were always good reasons for *nebbich* as well as for Jessasmarandjosef. We were middle-class people who had become proletarians, *nebbich*, and neither Jesus, Mary, nor Joseph wanted to take pity on us. Jews weren't spoken of, although everything connected with my origin was known to me. They concealed nothing from me, but things Jewish were not a topic of conversation.

After our move from the Upper Austrian province to Vienna, where antisemitism was a reality and the swastika a threat, my learning process began. I read everything I could turn up: from Langbehn to Moeller van den Bruck and Hans Blüher, from Houston Stewart Chamberlain and—more's the pity—even the conqueror of interest serfdom, Gottfried Feder, to Rosenberg's *Mythus des XX. Jahrhunderts* and also Hitler's *Mein Kampf*. I absorbed all of this foulness in an extremely ambivalent state. On the one hand, it was becoming clear to me that in their minds and hearts these people had made all the preparations for plunging me and my kind into ruin (thus I read with hate and hostile agitation); on the other hand, I still wanted to remain "objective" at all costs. I suppressed my burning anger and imposed on myself an intellectual calm that I have long since recognized as nothing but an element of psychic repression. It was an entirely impossible *éducation sentimentale* for a young Jew . . . Jew? Well, yes. Gradually, I began to understand that I myself, as a Jew, was my subject, although as chance and milieu would have it, I had but little contact with "genuine" Jews, Jews who were politically alert and fully conscious of their problems. Did I avoid their company? I must confess that I don't know anymore. All of that lies in life's distant past, and I can no longer be sure what was half-conscious choice in my social behavior and what was fate. When I was nineteen years old, so I now believe, my entire spiritual structure was still a product of the dull provinces.

In the summer of 1932—Papen was already at the helm in Germany and clerico-fascism was already a threat in Austria—a decisive event took place that for me was weightier than all my good and bad reading, all my helplessness and provinciality: I fell in love with the girl who was later to become my first wife. She had the snow-white, lightly freckled skin of a true redhead, a tiny, turned-up nose, and a very beautiful large mouth with perfect teeth. She was eighteen, came from Graz, and spoke a dialect that was very close to my native one. She wore Austrian folk dress, so-called dirndls, which became her marvelously well. When it turned out that she was a full-blooded, professing Jew, even that her Styrian origin was not untainted, and that her father was an immigrant *Ostjude*, my whole world collapsed. "Das ist ein polnisches Judenmädchen," said my mother, who regarded every woman with whom I happened to be involved as a loathsome troublemaker anyhow.

Despite maternal protest, I didn't give up the fair-skinned girl, but I ignored her background. I wanted by all means to be an anti-Nazi, that most certainly, but of my own accord; I was not yet ready to take Jewish destiny upon myself. Why not? Well, it is clear: By reading so many national-socialist works, I had allowed the enemy to impose his image of my self upon me and had completely internalized it—as Sartre was to explain in his unsurpassable *Anti-Semite and Jew*. I wanted to oppose the Nazis and merrily joined in the scuffles that were constantly going on back then at Vienna University. But it was to be a decision made freely, and not because of "blood" or "race." So it happened that at the same time as I was already turning away from Carossa and reading Feuchtwanger instead, I perfected my mimicry, which at bottom really wasn't that—since, after all, I was actually not lacking in idiotic nativeness. My hair was blond, my eyes were blue, and I very successfully lent them a menacing flash. My thoroughly Jewish nose, inherited directly from grandfather, still did not have that unequivocal severity that it fortunately took on later and that *marked* me. I really found myself in a confusing state of mind: I was an Austrian who had been raised as a Christian, and yet I was not one. Not any longer. The overwhelming majority not only of the German people but also of my own Austrian people had excluded me from their community. I should have been able to accept this already then— if only I had been ready to accept the *truth*. But what was that, the truth? Was it hidden in mother's Jessasmarandjosef, in the memories of midnight mass and high mass, in my dialect, in grandfather's Vorarlberg family tree, or in my Jewish nose? When I try to reflect on this question today, I must in a very precise sense give due to the nose. Even for the distant past, which I now view differently.

I know that the word "race" is taboo. But only a fool can deny that there are human races and that these manifest themselves not only in physical characteristics (dark, fair, reddish skin color, etc.) but also in psychic and intellectual ones. I have no proof for it and am also aware that modern biologists would hardly want to accept my opinion. But in the end, do not the experiences of a long life count more than a few disputed laboratory papers that tomorrow will perhaps lead to totally different hypotheses? I am certain, and no current anthropological claim will shake this certainty, that my intellect and my spiritual constitution are Jewish—not in the sense of upbringing or milieu, which in my case were as un-Jewish as possible, but by birth. And now let whoever wants to call me a nasty "racist"!

But I've jumped ahead in my chronology. It is absolutely necessary to mention a date that was crucial for me: 1935. The Nuremberg Reich Citizenship Law, about which I read in a Vienna coffee house and whose text I soon knew by heart, finally made it completely clear to me that for the Nazis—and not just for the most rabid of them but rather for the majority of all Germans and Austrians—I was a Jew, or, as it said: "I was considered a Jew." Once I tried reading the history of the Jews by Graetz, but it bored me. That is where things have remained until today; this too must be confessed. My knowledge of biblical events is limited to Thomas Mann's Joseph tetralogy. My view of history is that of the average European who calls himself "educated" but who, as Robert Musil once said so delightfully of himself, is merely "broadly uneducated." That is: there are gigantic gaps in this view that I never really took the pains to fill in. The story of the Chosen People is one of them. Only once in my life, in the icy cold winter of 1940–41, while interned by the French at Gurs in the Pyrenees, I attended an orthodox Jewish Chanukah celebration. Hearing the gripping, sorrowful cries to which the singsong of the worshippers intensified, I felt that I had been cast into another, thoroughly alien world. Standing next to me was the philosopher Georg Grelling. We looked at one another speechlessly and, alas, also somewhat ashamed. The fine gentleman from Berlin cleared his throat and said with embarrassment: "It's like in the Ethnological Museum." To the extent that I, as an atheist, grappled with the phenomenon of religion at all (and "grappled" is already saying too much), it was Christianity that stirred my interest. This is really not so incomprehensible. For to be a "Christian" doesn't mean only to believe in God and His Son. To be a questioning Christian doesn't mean that all one does is to clarify theological problems for oneself. It means *participation* in our culture. The ecclesia was always a presence for me; the synagogue was the Other. For this reason I cannot truly speak of my "Judaism." I propose another concept that I am firmly convinced is weightier, a concept I declare myself to be an expert on, unconditionally and without concession: *Being a Jew*. At which point I can resume my earlier presentation in its proper chronology.

In 1935, I learned of and permanently internalized the Nuremberg Laws. My *being a Jew* became clear to me. What it meant for me at that moment gradually intensified in a frightening way due to my later experiences, but it has not actually changed qualitatively. Society decreed that I was a Jew; I had to accept the sentence. A retreat into subjectivity, which might have allowed me to claim that I didn't "feel" Jewish, would have been an irrelevant, private game. Only a decade later did I read in Sartre's *Anti-Semite and Jew* that the Jew is someone whom the others regard as a Jew. This was precisely my case.

When the thunderbolt struck, when on March 11, 1938, my country threw itself exultantly into the arms of the Führer of the pan-Germanic Reich like a bitch in heat that just can't wait, I was ready. To be sure, one obstacle still had to be cleared: my mother. On the sly, she had taken care of everything. Her first fiancé, a flawlessly aryan gentleman, was ready to swear that in truth I was *his* child, and not that of my fully Jewish father. And a friend of the family's, who had an important position at the Family Research Office, would straighten out the matter. For my part, I needed only to take care of a trifle in a hurry: part from my Jewish girl, who meanwhile had become my lawful wife. Even today I still ask myself, and find no answer, whether I would not have agreed to Mother's proposal if I had been less passionately attached to this dialect-speaking Jewish girl, who would have cut the best figure as a model for the tourism offices of the "Ostmark."

I would like to say proudly: Certainly not; and I would have left my country even without having to, as an emigrant for reasons of principle. How incompatible are pride and honesty! The latter forbids me the former and I can only say: I don't know what would have happened if . . . I still wasn't familiar with the concept of "authenticity" that became so common after the war. But perhaps I vaguely felt nonetheless that a human being cannot exist within a total lie, one that encompasses his entire person, his entire life. I constituted myself as a Jew. Certainly, there were still hurdles I didn't know how to take. At no cost, for example, did I want the mandatory middle name "Israel" to be inscribed into my papers; I didn't get myself a passport because they would have stamped the red "J" into it.

In Antwerp, the first station of flight, it was the "Joodse Komiteit" that looked after us. He who had never lived among Jews was now surrounded by Jews exclusively, all of whom had nothing else on their minds—society saw to that!—than their being Jewish. As they said back then in the current jargon, there was now a "community of fate." There was a "national community." It stood the test. For the wealthy Jewish community of Antwerp took care of us as though we were its children. As for me, it was just as ugly as it was stupid when more than once I reacted with the most extreme irritation to the fellowship that surrounded me. The Yiddish language, in which I was addressed everywhere, was an unspeakable embarrassment for me. To be sure, I had accepted my being Jewish as a *principle*, but in daily practice I failed. I felt vaguely that I would have to pass through other, harder schools in order really to be what I was: a Jew. The teachers and taskmasters were already on the way.

On May 10, 1940, when the Germans began their general offensive across the western border, I—a "German citizen"—was arrested as an enemy alien. They took us deep into southern France. In vain did we emigrants try to make clear to the Belgian and French guards that we were not enemies of the allies, that we weren't Germans, but Jews. These people understood nothing. Jews? What does that mean? Jewishness is a religion. Léon Blum is also a Jew. We had nothing to do with Blum, we were "des boches." But when France was defeated in six weeks, the heads of the French seemed suddenly to have cleared up in a fabulous way. The "boches," that is, the real Germans, looked after by Hitler's Truce Commissions, were freed and admired as victors by the French in a most repulsively servile manner. We others, the refugees, unwanted in the Reich, were instantly transformed from the enemy into burdensome aliens and above all: into Jews, now in the full sense of the German racist notion. "Sale juif" superseded the abusive "sale boche." The aversion against the Jews, as it seemed to me, certainly must have lain in much deeper strata of the French nature than their superficial "anti-bochisme." The Jewish identity imposed on me by society—I could feel it more strongly every day—was no German phenomenon. It was not only the Nazis who turned me into a Jew. The world insisted that I be one, and I was ready to do what Sartre later called "assumer," freely and inadequately translated, "to take upon oneself." I wrested from myself the feeling of solidarity with *every* Jew. We were already locked into the ghetto, and it was like the one in which the world has enclosed the tiny state of Israel today.

Soon the teachers changed. The innocently brutal Gardes Mobiles who had insulted us in the Gurs internment camp disappeared—after I had broken out of the camp for the sake of my wife and beloved, hiked through half of France, and was again in German-occupied Belgium—the Master-of-Death from Germany had taken their place. The Résistance, which I joined in a most modest capacity and entirely without heroic emotional gestures, became, if I think about it today, my last, perhaps even only unconscious attempt to evade the Jewish identity that I had long since taken upon myself intellectually. The Jews were hunted, cornered, arrested, deported *because they were Jews*, and only because of that. Looking back, it appears to me that I didn't want to be detained by the enemy as a Jew but rather as a resistance member. It was my last, absurd effort to escape a collective fate. Thus, I distributed ineffective flyers at the risk of my life but with the falsely proud consciousness that I was a "fighter" and not one of those who, bleating like sheep, allowed themselves to be led to the slaughter bench.

But after my arrest, reality immediately caught up with me. I was highly interesting to the bloodhounds as long as they thought I was a German deserter, soldier, perhaps even officer. When they became aware of my identity they threw me onto the dungheap. "Troop demoralization" was marked into my file, and as long as the fellows believed I was a deserter they submitted me to highly discomforting interrogations. When they realized who I was, I lost all relevance for them. There was no trial. I was subjected to the general death sentence; it was called *Auschwitz*. Can anything be added to what I have already recorded in my book *At the Mind's Limits?* Perhaps only this: In Auschwitz my being a Jew assumed the final form that it has retained until today. While I had been arrested as a Résistance member, in Auschwitz I wore the yellow star and was a Jew like all those others who had never dared even to kick, let alone distribute seditious flyers. In the circle of hell the differences really did become perceptible and burned themselves into our skin like the tatoo numbers with which they marked us. In the abyss, all of the "aryan" prisoners were on a level so far *above* us, the Jews, that it can be measured only in light-years. They beat us when it pleased them; especially the Poles distinguished themselves at this, in a way that is unforgettable and should not be concealed. They had all internalized the Führer's values—because tradition had trained them for it. They may have been destined to be slaves of the master race; but we were signed over to death. It reached the point where we Jews allowed ourselves to be beaten without resistance. Only once did I strike back, in the mistaken belief that in this way I could regain my human dignity. Then I recognized that it made no sense. The Jew was the sacrificial animal. He had to drink the cup, down to its bitter end. I drank. And this became my Jewish being. *Judaism* was another matter. I had nothing to do with it. I learned to understand Yiddish but made no effort to speak it. Now and then it happened that Eastern European Jews gathered and sang Yiddish songs, whose texts I halfway understood. It moved me deeply when a few of them once joined into a Zionist song with the refrain: "Iach fuhr aheim"—"I'm going home." "Aheim," for them that was the Holy Land. Home, homeland, for me they would remain words without meaning. I was at home nowhere. I was a Jew and I wanted, and was, to remain one. After my return to Belgium in 1945, when I was becoming more and more interested in French culture and fell in love with the city of Paris, when Jean-Paul Sartre became something of a "father figure" for me, I no longer believed in assimilation. How could it have even been possible? I had never been "assimilated," but rather I had been fully Austrian like anyone else. And still Jewish fate had overtaken me. How could I have now imagined—resurrected but more vulnerable than ever—that there was even the slightest glimmer of hope of my becoming a Frenchman? It was not because of the language. What made it impossible for me to invent a new present were the memories of childhood and youth, which formed my past and at the same time were no longer valid; they were destroyed and had long since decayed, but they still existed negatively. The exile-in-permanence that I chose was the sole authenticity I could attain for myself; being Jewish blocked all other outlets for me.

To be sure I had not acquired *Judaism* in the sense of historical tradition and a positive existential foundation of life. The only thing that binds me positively to the majority of Jews in the world is a solidarity that I have long since not had to enjoin on myself as a duty: solidarity with the state of Israel. Not that I would want to live in this country. It is too hot for me, too loud, too foreign in every respect. Also it is not that I approve of everything they do there. I detest the theocratic tendencies, the religiously tinged nationalism. I have also seen the country only once on a short visit and perhaps will never get there again. But even if I don't speak their language and their way of life could never be mine, I am inseparably bound to the people of this tragic land, who are alone, abandoned by the entire world. For me Israel is no promised land, no territorial claim legitimized by the Bible, no Holy Land, but rather a gathering place of survivors, a political entity in which every single inhabitant, still and for a long time to come, must fear for his physical existence. For me, solidarity with Israel means keeping faith with my dead comrades.

Ever anew I make the attempt to distance myself. But I can never completely succeed. I am an alert critic of Israeli policies; I don't hesitate to forfeit good will, to jeopardize friendships if I openly and sharply reject the present government of Israel as being irrationally and chauvinistically inspired. I say aloud that I am opposed to the man Begin and all he stands for. But when it is suddenly a matter of do or die and I sense danger for the little land that is desperately trying to defend itself, then—beyond a Judaism to which I can lay no claim since I don't possess it—my *being Jewish* is in the end decisive after all. I take sides. *For* Israel—and I barely shrug my shoulders when my friends from the Left call me a renegade. They have it easy: loyalty to principles is child's play. I make things hard for myself. For loyalty to fate, to which I submit, is an unclear concept, and whoever holds to it must jettison all convenient theories, all crutches of dogma; he stands on shaky ground. No God will help him, and no Marx. Least of all, a Hegel.

He can turn, *I* can turn, to nothing except experience, the quality of which is incommunicable. When the land of Israel, for me not a holy land, is threatened, I see flames everywhere. And I shout: Fire! I know that my cry fades away unheard. Those who are rooted in *Judaism* dispute my right to be heard, and in this they are logical. The others, who never experienced the threat as a personal, physical one, don't listen anyhow. I cannot condemn them since I myself do not think daily about the massacre of the Armenians by the Turks. People talk about politics and history, objective events. I remain fixed to experience, to the bitter end. If I could claim Judaism as my own I could quickly turn subjective experience into objective, finalistic historicity. This path is closed to me. Four walls are closing in, the room is becoming smaller. *Being Jewish* (which I didn't choose) without a *Judaism* (which descent and early surroundings would permit me to choose only at the price of an existential lie) leads to a melancholy that I must live through daily; a melancholy that accompanies my existence and would most likely be designated by specialists as "neurotic," but that I regard as the sole frame of mind to which I am entitled.

In the Waiting Room of Death

Reflections on the Warsaw Ghetto

TO BEGIN WITH, the question of qualification: "People in the Ghetto"—who has the right to talk about them? Everyone, as long as the intention is an objective portrayal of *how* it really was. But if one abandons the historiographical terrain and strives for something that can be called, unclearly and perhaps a bit ostentatiously, the phenomenology of the victim's existence in the ghetto, if one aims for reflection that must be based on direct experience but that is to be extracted from its immediacy and filtered through the medium of thought—then above all others those are qualified who experienced the events in person.

The author of this introduction already feels uncertain, for he was not in the ghetto himself. But perhaps he can turn to an admissible metaphor and state: Since the enactment of the Nuremberg Laws the ghetto caught up with every Jew ("Jews: persons regarded as Jews according to the Reich Citizenship Law of September 15, 1935 . . ."), even if earlier he had shared the dream of assimilation and casually brushed off his Jewish identity. But, sad privilege that it is, I need not

"Im Warteraum des Todes"; first published as the introduction to a volume of photographs from the Warsaw Ghetto, *Menschen im Ghetto* (People in the ghetto), ed. Günther Deschner (Gütersloh: Bertelsmann Sachbuchverlag, 1969), pp. 11–31.

base my attempt at justification only on a metaphorically extended ghetto experience: Two years in the concentration camps, of them a year in Auschwitz, may, indeed must, suffice. Behind the electrically charged barbed wire I and others like me had experiences that were probably not basically different from those of the ghetto inmates. Perhaps only our dread was not as great since we had, after all, already left the Waiting Room of Death, and the ghetto dwellers were still cowering in it. Our train had already arrived. What those behind the ghetto walls had feared was already reality for us.

Still another attempt to revive the horrors? One has already had enough of all that, right? It is all very familiar. The ghetto—and then what? Dresden is thrown into the discussion, and Hiroshima, and Vietnam, and—who knows—perhaps even the homes of the Palestinians blown up by Jewish commandos. Man is not good; that's the way it was, it is, and will be, and history is not the teacher but the torturer of mankind. What the ghetto was like? This way and that. Bad, of course. But why stir up the past, etc. Perhaps that is why it is good to tell what it was: so that the How can achieve its specific dimension, and historical detachment may feel shame at its nice objectivity.

Let me repeat the phrase "Waiting Room of Death," even though it can be objected that this metaphor borders somewhere on the journalistic. But, just a moment! The ghetto, the Nazi-German ghetto that we are talking about here *was* the anteroom of death; and whether the metaphor is journalistic or not, it is totally congruent with the reality experienced in an accursed time. Not every ghetto was comparable to the one invented and structured by the Nazis. The ghettos that separated Jews from Christians from the late Middle Ages into the eighteenth century were prisons, certainly; and in this regard they were hardly different from the Warsaw Ghetto. But it must never be forgotten that they were at the same time also a kind of home for the homeless.

For the Jew the historical ghetto was not only spatial separation, which he felt to be a dishonor, but his consciously *lived* separation from the Christians, who ate impure food and worshipped an un-God. It was the topographical counterpart of a mental and religious attitude. In addition, the Jews in the historical ghetto were more or less secure—to the extent that Jews could be secure at all. What was it that Klabund once wrote?

On Sunday a word is dropped in church
On Monday it snowballs through the streets
On Tuesday they talk of racial hate
On Wednesday the roar is heard: pogrom![1]

Close enough. Murder, burning houses, torture, and rape were a danger but killing was not an absolute, unavoidable certainty. One could escape it through flight, through servility, through baptism, also with the help of money. Hope was not forbidden. "Next year in Jerusalem," that was the ritualized illusion. But it was not madness. Death lay as a shadow over the historical ghetto; it was not yet decreed as ineluctable. In the Nazi ghetto it was different, completely and totally different, even if in the end one or the other did manage to survive and even if there were a few whom the wind swept to Jerusalem like drifting sand. There could be no hope. Put differently and more correctly—since the theological concept of hope in its immanent-transcendental ambiguity obscures the real state of affairs: There could no longer be any trust in the world when all were forced to see daily that not only the improbable was taking place but also what until then had been deemed completely impossible. The ghetto wall was also the demarcation line that separated the Jew from the *human being*. The latter, even in his crippled form as an oppressed Pole, was permitted in principle to live—as a slave, to be sure, without schools, without civil rights, without dignity, if you will; but he was not prevented from breathing. The oppressed non-Jew could be expelled, deported, thrown into prison, in certain circumstances—and they occurred only too often!—murdered. But he knew precisely and made no secret of it when associating with Jews, that a world separated him from them: the insane world of the Nazi race theory. Thus the total solitude of the Ghetto Jew.

This solitude is not that of the colonized, about which a man like Frantz Fanon tells us when describing the condition of the Algerians under French rule. To be sure, what Fanon said of the colonial slave holds true also for the Jew: that the master "makes" the servant and thereby determines him in his entire being. However, the colonial master "makes" his dehumanized human workhorse for the purpose of exploitation, and the clear, immanent law of exploitation demands in turn that everything be taken from the exploited but that his life be spared. For the Nazi, on the other hand, the death of the Jew, the

Final Solution, took uncontestable priority over exploitation. The Ghetto Jews were made to work until they died like dogs. Decisive, however, was not their work but their death. For this reason, the answer given by the Ghetto Jew—given to himself, to his existence, his master, and the world—was necessarily a different one. "The glance that the colonized cast on the town of the colonial master," Fanon says, "was a glance of lustful envy. The dream of possession, of all manner of possession: to sit down at the table of the colonial master, to sleep in his bed, if possible, with the master's wife." The dream of the Ghetto Jew did not go that far. He did not wish to wear the SS man's smart uniform. Because he despised the Death's Head Priest, one can object, and would be partly right in doing so. But just partly! If the Jew in the Nazi-German ghetto so seldom reached the point of a hate that was fraught with envy, of the dream of possession, it was because he was unable to summon the necessary strength. He had internalized the image of himself created by the Nazi; he had become the louse of Kafka's *Metamorphosis*. From what remained of the religious conceit of chosenness and his faulty knowledge of talmudic wisdom he despised the blond "German woman"; but he also revered her and did not even dream of approaching her rosy body. His reaction was fear and flight. His history—which will not be discussed here, since its basic elements are common knowledge—had prepared him for the role that the Nazi forced him to play to its very last consequences. His unspeakable solitude was also determined by flight and fear. The fugitive does not have a good, or even a bad, comrade; the sole comrade of the person driven by fear is his fear. To introduce a concept that was developed by Sartre in the *Critique of Dialectical Reason*, he and his companions in fate belonged to the "series" and not to a "group." Hence the peculiar dialectic of Jewish solidarity, which realized itself in *suffering*—no matter what Frau Hannah Arendt may have told us in her remarkably uncomprehending Eichmann book, which does not even contain relevant factual knowledge—in suffering, and only in rare instances in a seemingly impossible struggle, which was doomed to failure from the start. The Jewish Kapos and block seniors, the Jewish ghetto police and base ghetto notables suffered along with their victims, despite everything. They beat their fellow Jew and in doing so were beating themselves. They drove him into the gas chambers and never once believed that they could save themselves by such betrayal. The solidarity that extends only to suffering and does not include struggle within its horizon is as miserable as the Nazi wanted the Jew to be.

If the historical ghetto—in which the Jew consciously separated himself from the Christian, who for him was a heathen—can be seen as the distorted form of Jewish national sovereignty, as a caricature of the Promised Land, if you will, then the Nazi-German ghetto was the realization of the mad Nazi dream of the Jewish subhuman, over whom the Nazi superman ruled for the sole purpose of finally killing him. The Nazi actually succeeded in creating "his" Jew according to his own distorted pattern. Could the Ghetto Jew do other than accommodate himself to the image that the superman desired? Become and die! the master commanded. The Jew, accustomed only to the world's hate, obeyed. He wailed, and struggled with his comrade in death for a spoonful of soup. He was nimble at black-marketeering. He had always manipulated money only—and, oh, how wretchedly little— and thus in the ghetto, too, he believed in the flimsy illusion of the unreliable possession of cash. He put on airs when it mattered, and had the band play a tango—which he knew to be the dance of death. At times it seemed as though he wanted to dupe and deride the Nazi: You wanted to have me so shameful! Take a look; I'm even more shameful, shameful to the point of complete absurdity, so that your design becomes a travesty and you yourself become a fool and are fooled. Weapons of flight and fear. One can scarcely talk of Jewish "collaboration," then! In the face of the ghetto all political and moral categories break down, become simply unusable. What the Nazis perpetrated on those concentrated in the Eastern ghettos lay far beyond all judgment. For what can one do with a concept like "cruelty," which can be used, after all, to describe the behavior of a spiteful sergeant! What can be done, I say, with everyday words when not only customary everyday reality was exceeded but when every day deeds were committed that will forever remain indescribable? Weapons of flight and fear, even they are ennobled in the face of the enemy. Who, of all those who were not there, dares to chime in and speak of the "lack of dignity" of a people that let itself be led to the slaughtering block "like a flock of sheep"? Yet, even if every response to the dehumanization process of the Nazis is legitimate and must be accepted (since the code of honor in the duel between the hunter and the hunted also includes the hare's agile double-back), let it be said that there is a hierarchy of responses. One person was a "collaborator" and enjoyed himself a bit before they got rid of him. The other armed himself with the wisdom of the victim and bowed down before the misdeeds of a God who was Moloch. The third died bravely, like a soldier, with no heroic act of resistance, certainly, but still as the helper of his weaker comrade. We esteem him more than the wise, hoary victim at his prayers, who in turn takes precedence over the clumsily heel-clicking chairman of some Jewish Council. But high above both stands the one who rebelled. The one who took up arms, mostly primitive arms, and opposed the highly technical battle equipment of the murderer, was . . . What? Well, at the risk of lapsing into a trivial formulation: He was the hero absolute. And one can only be amazed, can only marvel at the great number of men and women who freed themselves not only from the ghetto but from a two-thousand year history—in the situation that had been readied for them, the situation of death, in which the upright person is already cut down while he still thinks he is in battle position. Resistance, violence, they were not the "solution"—there was no other but the one planned at the Wannsee Conference!—but no matter how futile, they were historically and humanly the most valuable responses and held most promise for the future. In his book *Treblinka* (of which, unfortunately, too little notice was taken in Germany), the young French author Jean-François Steiner, probably the sole person to have attained a visionary grasp of the situation in the ghetto and death camp without having been "on the spot," has one of the protagonists say: "I don't want to live, I want to take revenge!" Indeed, in deliberations devoted to the men and women in the Waiting Room of Death one cannot omit the problem of revenge, or more concretely, of avenging violence that is intended as the nullification of the oppressor's violence. Let us not forget that the history of the Warsaw Ghetto culminated in an armed insurrection that militarily was wholly absurd and can be justified only morally, as the realization of *humane vengeance*. In revolt, that of Warsaw or also that in Treblinka, the Ghetto Jew, while totally preserving his qualities, transcended himself and attained to an entirely new ontic dimension. He was the prey who bore within him a two-thousand-year history of humiliation. But for one moment he became the hunter, not for the joy of hunting but from the will to remain who he was and at the same time to become another. The history of the revolts in the ghetto and in various camps permits us to see how things really were. In the numerous documentary works, to which nothing need be added here, we read that it was by no means only heroes who became heroes there, who took up iron bars and set out with them against tanks. The nimble black-marketeer was there, the scholar who still the day before, while studying the Scriptures, was determined to offer himself up as a compliant victim, the brutal ghetto policeman, some Jewish Council's list-compiling bookkeeper for slaughter-cattle, the socialist, accustomed from early on to the thought of physical resistance, the simply apprehensive father of a family. They had been lost in the "series" and now closed ranks in a "group." The group-forming agent was the determination for revenge. What an unpopular term is being introduced here! I already hear protests: No, that's not the way it was! An eye for an eye, a tooth for a tooth, jus talionis; for God's sake, that is by no means what the Jews wanted who were rousing themselves to resistance!

Yes, it is! I believe that is what they wanted. I myself, the author of this contribution, wanted just that; and countless comrades along with me. That they and I did not rise in revolt remains our very painful, constantly reopening wound. Certainly, the Jew as the Nazi saw him and forced him to see himself was not suited for that. He told the sad joke about two Jews who, sometime around 1943, were talking about the coming days of the allied victory. One of them says: You know, I picture it like this. I'm sitting, as I used to, in the coffee house, a stack of liberal newspapers in front of me. Who comes in but Hitler—small, bent, shabby, humble. He comes up to my table and asks: Excuse me, might there be a paper available? And I look at him over the top of my glasses and say politely but firmly: Not for *you!*

This was the reaction of the Jews according to Nazi design: Fear and flight were carried over into the time of freedom, and revenge consisted only in ridicule and painful shame. It was reserved for few to discover their authenticity in battle and in genuine revenge. For few and many. For the power of the oppressor—dividing and ruling, in the end decreeing inescapable death—had succeeded in destroying the practical, the psychological, and the existential foundations of the human act of vengeance.

It must be recognized and appreciated that this vengeance was not a cocky, romantic vendetta in the Romance tradition, nor was it the comparatively simple "violence" that Fanon, or Che Guevara, or Regis Debray proposed for the battle of the colonized and oppressed. As little as the Jew fixed his gaze with "lustful envy," as did Fanon's colonized man, onto the homestead of the oppressor—since, after all, he both despised and respected the master—that is how little his actually hopeless revenge could be the violence and revolution of the Algerian or the black-skinned American. For him more was at stake, and it was something different, something that elsewhere I myself termed—inappropriately, as I now realize—the "reattainment of dignity." Because in an act of sudden freedom, only a few minutes before its time, he snatched to himself what was nothing but certain death; because he was *alone*, completely and despairingly alone; because as the reward for his violence, and this is the decisive point, he could not, like the Algerian, expect liberation; his revenge had to have a completely different existential character.

What kind was it? Well, this much is clear: it had the character of authentication and the free acceptance of a situation that in its lack of any freedom was entirely unacceptable. The "reattainment of dignity" was indeed an inadequate formulation. For what is usually called dignity could not be taken from anyone by the Nazi, nor by anybody else. An entire history of persecution, insanely anchored in the notion of deicide, was unable to rob the Jew of his dignity, whether it was the money-lending Jew, or the talmudist, or the great Jewish poet and scholar. As concerns Jewish revenge, or the violence of counterviolence upon which he decided literally at the last moment in the concentration camp or in the ghetto, what makes it so singular and irreducible was *the freedom of choosing death*, which was opposed to death as a decree of the enemy and made into reality. Was it suicide? Naturally, it was that too. But what differentiated it from real suicide, which one can regard as the final and most consistent form of the flight-and-fear reaction, was the ultimate fact that the ring of total isolation had been broken: death was not only suffered but also meted out. Here the redemptory application of violence had been found in its purest form. Here revenge was cleansed of a Christian moralism that was never able to prevent it, that always merely denied it. Here and here alone, as far as we can survey history, the dreadful and, in all its dreadfulness, empty phrase about "cleansing the ignominy through blood" made good sense.

But I've jumped ahead. Revolt and avenging, liberating force were the final aim, the historic and moral goal that was not attained often enough. They were the utopia that was only occasionally realized. Chronologically, too, they lay at the end of a long journey through the night. It will be necessary to return to what was for every Jew the irreplaceable existential *value* of consummated revenge, which—it dare not be forgotten for a second—was never carried out on the defenseless but on a heavily armed oppressor. There will also be discussion further on of the task that was fulfilled in the insurrection and without which perhaps a state like Israel would be unthinkable. First, however, we want to return to the point where, in the haste to progress to something brighter, we left the ghetto with quick step, so to speak, and were searching for the revolutionary situation, for the anti-ghetto. In reality, as everyone knows, there was little fighting and much suffering in the ghetto, and a description of the essence of ghetto existence must in the end adhere more to the sluggish hours, days, months, years of suffering than to the moment of revolt and transcendence.

What is there to add that would go beyond the rather thorough documentation already available? Too much and too little. Too much to be mastered here in the abundance of its material. Too little to illuminate entirely new formal-philosophical aspects. Perhaps there are only isolated phenomena that are not yet known well enough so that it may be worthwhile pointing them out. First of all—and I am now speaking from my own concentration camp experiences as well as my study of the ghetto literature—there was the physical compression of human masses within the most confining space. In the ghetto Sartre's all-too-often quoted words: "L'enfer, c'est les autres"—"Hell, that is the others," took on a very concrete sense that was felt bodily. The victims were not only made into a "series" by their oppressor; since they constantly saw, smelled, and touched one another, they were physically deindividualized and made into an opaque *mass* of flesh. Whoever reads about the ghetto and then reads something pseudoclever or even genuinely clever about our modern "mass civilization" must let out a bitter laugh. Masses, "mass man"—that is not the television viewer in his single-family home, even if he is exposed to the pressure of the mass media. The ghetto dweller had physically become one with the mass, at the same time that he was battling senselessly and desperately against the other cells of this mass of flesh. The ghetto was a malignant tumor of humanity. Every single one of those crammed into it understood it as such and felt himself to be the sick cell of an organism, which, objectively, he really was. Therefore, he could love himself as little as he could the next person. For one another—and here again I am speaking from my own camp experience, which may legitimately be applied to the ghetto—we were nothing but disgust. Self-disgust then emerged of necessity, since everyone sensed that for his fellow sufferer he was merely someone who was eating the bread that could have been his, taking the air he needed to breathe, the space for moving about. But where self-love and loving communication with one's fellow man were blocked, there could hardly emerge the so urgently needed, total, unconditional hate for the antiman, hate that was ready to employ violence, ready for revenge. Nothing remained except, again and again, the already mentioned solidarity of suffering, a solidarity that was incapable of love and joy projected outward, or of resistance—which in common colloquial language can more or less be reduced to the formula: "You're a poor dog just like me!" A *poor* dog, certainly, but a dog. Throughout times of relative freedom also, this mentality of self-disgust had accompanied the Jew, who, coming from the historical ghetto, after the all too brief historical period of emancipation was thrown back into the Nazi-German ghetto, the inhospitable Waiting Room of Death. One is familiar with the profound "e'soi" joke, which no less a writer than Arthur Schnitzler included in his great novel on the Jewish Question, *The Road to the Open.* An Orthodox Jew is sitting in a train compartment opposite a properly dressed gentleman, whom he takes to be a Christian. He decorously draws in his legs, scarcely dares to clear his throat. Suddenly the proper gentleman takes a Hebrew newspaper from his pocket and begins to read. Whereupon the Orthodox Jew breathes a sigh of relief: "E'soi" (Aha!)—and stretches his legs out onto the opposite seat . . . The poor dog in European disguise sitting across from the Orthodox Jew deserved no better treatment. In the Nazi-German ghetto, where, to boot, the bodily crowding-together of the Jews excluded mutual respect, this mentality became paroxysmal.

On such a social foundation, or, better yet, in the true sense of the word, asocial foundation, there now arose in the ghetto, as there did by the way in the concentration camp also, an economic structure that was nothing other than the capitalistic economic system raised to the degree of self-nullification, self-caricature, and absurdity. It was the triumph of a capitalistic Social Darwinism, which was joined—to a lesser extent in the ghetto than in the concentration camp, but still visibly enough—by the law of the physically strongest. Among the very weakest of this earth, he was strong who possessed money, who knew how to get hold of it, if need be, by exerting superior physical strength. A hierarchy arose, whereas what should have mattered most was that no poor dog be more and better than the next, so that together they could become a wolf pack of full equals.

Concealed in this hierarchy lay something extremely enigmatic: hope amidst hopelessness. Everyone hoped that the great broom that was cleaning up might pass him by. No one really believed in this hope. "The whole truth is," Hannah Arendt wrote, "that if the Jewish people [not only in the ghetto but in all of Nazi-occupied territory] had really been without a leader, there would have been chaos and victims and much misery, but the total number of victims would hardly have been between four and a half and six million people." That has been contested by the most authoritative sources, and it appears rather absurd to me also. But one thing is certain: the "leaders" of this people, in the ghetto above all the Jewish Council and the Jewish police, would have done better not to cling to that unbelieved-in and hopeless hope, but from the start to entrust their cause and that of their charges to nothing and no one. In this case, that means to expect nothing but their own death, which had to come in any event, and to prepare for the avenging use of violence.

What prevented them from acting in this way was apparently the habit of suffering in silence, fixed for two millennia, or, as it has been formulated here, the fear-and-flight reaction, which had become a character constituent. In this context, the answer that Martin Buber once gave in a letter to Gandhi after "Kristallnacht" seems inferior. The latter had tried to convince Buber that the German Jews would do better to sacrifice their lives on the altar of passive resistance in order thereby to awaken world conscience. Hereupon Buber replied to the Mahatma that such a voluntary martyrdom was senseless, especially since Judaism did not "teach death but rather life." This argument, which is quite ridiculous in view of the genuine religion of death in the Nazi-German ghetto, later was put forth in connection with the controversy over Hannah Arendt's Eichmann book. If I am not mistaken and have not falsely interpreted my own concentration camp experiences, it was by no means the Jewish "precept of life" that paradoxically permitted the masses of Jews to go to their death without resistance; rather, it was the fear-and-flight reaction, which had become a collective basic character trait, enforced, to be sure, by the humanly corrupting social structure of the ghetto. The corruption process of the Nazis has been referred to often enough, so that here just a few allusions may serve as a reminder. It was the Nazis who erected the caricature-like capitalistic system combined with the right of the strongest (although it was supported by the Jewish merchant tradition), in which the mobility of money held out the security that the native population found in house and home. It was the Nazis who constantly nourished hopes that they destroyed at the next moment, only to fan them again a moment later. In the ghetto and concentration camp one could cherish the illusion that one could survive by working one's way up (at the cost of self-surrender) into the ranks of the ghetto or camp notables.

The Nazi caused the poor dog-of-a-Jew to hope; and he hoped as a hoping person, even if he never trusted his hope. The Nazis gave every Jew the chance to become a scoundrel, writes Jean-François Steiner. To be sure, and it is important for me to repeat this, the concept of scoundrel hardly retained any meaning in the ghetto. Every answer to the Nazi's crushing of the Jews' humanity was legitimate in the ghetto—also the answer that, in the usual sense, was most base. Only thoughtlessness, brazen arrogance, and complete ignorance of the situation can condemn the "collaborationist Jew" like some Quisling in occupied Europe! Certainly, the Nazi had seen to it that, if you wish, too many Jews took advantage of the chance to become a scoundrel; but in the excess of terror that he had organized he brought it about, very much against his will, that even the lowest Jewish villain was no longer a villain. In a very definite sense, he had forever elevated a people that he wanted not only to destroy physically but to turn morally and historically into an antipeople. (It does not help the Neo-Nazis a bit when they say that the Jews want to blackmail the world with their millions of victims! For a long time to come, the world will have to submit to this pressure, which is anything but shabby coercion.)

Here, a further point must be included in the discussion, which we want to direct against all those people who in our judgment understand the phenomenology of the ghetto as little as they do its psychology and sociology. In some places the attempt was made to understand and explain the ghetto against the background of the very general phenomenon of "totalitarianism," more or less as though it had been nothing but the apotheosis of totalitarian rule. Anyone inclined to espouse such an interpretation is referred, to begin with, to Erwin

Leiser's magnificent film *Mein Kampf*, which presents montages of original film photography from the Warsaw Ghetto. In the ghetto, unlike in the totalitarian state, no one could save his life by submissiveness. What threatened him was not the arbitrariness of the police state that characterizes the "ordinary" totalitarian regime. Oh yes, Hitler, Himmler, and their accomplices had made choices according to their will, but all too simply and all too ruthlessly and generally for the concept of arbitrariness in its everyday usage to have any meaning. The conceptual world of politics as well as of morality had been invalidated by an excess of injustice. The triumph of radical evil (not "so-called" evil, which could be traced back to historical ethnic factors, and also not "banal" evil, in whose existence I can no longer believe) had permitted a world to arise in the ghetto that was not beyond, but certainly below, good and evil. This world had precious little to do with totalitarianism or dictatorship, or, in general, any historically known form of social community. It was very simply the contradictory reality of an antiworld or, if you wish, a world of death. Death had already invaded its waiting room. The Jewish "precept of life" was entirely powerless against it. Where it attempted to assert itself in the form of a false hope of survival, it only disclaimed itself; and the chance survival of this or that individual had nothing to do with the fundamental negation of life and ultimately of all morality in the service of life.

The dialectical paradox lay in the fact that whoever wished to preserve the principle of life in the ghetto had to accept death; that whoever was to restore morality at all had to include the obviously evil, that is, revenge, in his system. Accept death, I say. By that, I naturally do not mean a sacrificial death, death suffered passively at the hand of the other, but death that the ghetto dweller took voluntarily into his own hands, that he inflicted on himself by bringing it to the enemy. The ghetto was an inverted world, or a world of inversions: whoever wanted to survive in it had to be prepared, and willing, to perish. The Nazi himself had established this world of negations. "Members of the intellectual professions, step forward! We need clerks, bookkeepers, chemists," is the way it went in the camp that I knew in those days. The "intellectuals" made haste, stepped forward in double time, stood at attention. Then they were assigned to work details charged with especially hard physical labor. The Nazi negated himself through the lie that he was constantly telling; he negated the other, whom he subjugated to the lie and tossed to the dead while he was still living.

This general negation by the Nazi was a negation of life, of man, even of himself. Most certainly it was a negation of the spirit, of morality, of justice, of truth, of courage (for even the most courageous Jew was treated like a miserable coward). It could be opposed only by a comprehensive counternegation. Negation of the negation: if ever and anywhere this was more than dubious dialectical acrobatics, it was in the Nazi-German ghetto! The total negation of the negation could be nothing other than armed uprising against the tormentor, the revolt or "great refusal" that knows it is without a chance and still declares its loyalty to itself. With that, we have arrived once more at the problem of resistance and insurrection. As stated already, it seldom occurred. But where it did manifest itself, it was for that reason all the more admirable and, in the long run, more effective. Thanks to the insurgent Jews in some of the camps, above all in the Warsaw Ghetto, today the Jew can again look at his own human face, as a human being. Jean-François Steiner writes in his book *Treblinka:* "He [a camp prisoner] still did not know how he should revolt, but daily the idea filled him more and more, and thus he gradually lost his fear and his cowardice." If it had only been a matter of overcoming physical fear of the oppressor! It was that too, no doubt, but it was by no means only that. The simple formula of the attainment of human dignity of manly honor far from suffices to tell what the uprising in the camp or ghetto was. I spoke above of the ghetto inmate's boundless *solitude*, which distinguished his condition from that of the colonized or someone else who was somehow being oppressed. When the Algerians began their war against the French occupiers under the leadership of nine men, they were not alone. Not only Tunisia and Morocco, as already independent North African states of the former French colonial territory, were with them, but the moral support of the entire non-French world was assured them, including that of a young American senator named John F. Kennedy.

The negroes of the United States, even when they employ the most extreme verbal and concrete weapons in the battle for their rights and identity, have on their side the sympathy of the Third World, the communist world, as well as considerable parts of the Western world. Not so the Jew in the Nazi-German ghetto. The Pole or Ukrainian, who was likewise engaged in the partisan struggle against the Germans, did not help him. The Jew could be happy if they did not attack him directly or denounce him. Also the democratic world, which was at war against Hitler, accorded him no help. On the contrary! The allies made use of every opportunity to give their people, who were by no means free of traditional antisemitism, the binding assurance that the war was not being conducted for the Jews—who were abandoned to death. As though it would have been a disgrace to want to hinder the murder of millions with armed force!

The Jew was alone with his task of negating the negation. Whether he fulfilled his mission or not, this lends him his ontically unique dimension and his historically ineffaceable quality. He had to raise himself from the ground without an arm to support him. In the end, that is what it all came down to. The violent uprising was the negation of the ghetto condition, the eradication of two thousand years of false solidarity in suffering, the restoration not of "dignity," but of humanity pure and simple; it was the avenging establishment of justice, the chance to create a new kingdom of man on earth.

Are all these words too lofty? Pathos, in the sense of suffering, sympathetic suffering of what was inconceivably suffered, is the sole permissible tone when one reports on the ghetto beyond mere documentation. For no matter where we may look in the vast field of history, nowhere had "la condition humaine," as André Malraux termed it, so terribly become the condition inhumaine.

The ghetto, at least so it seems to me at this moment, was the beginning of the end of Jewish history as the story of the sufferer. Since the Nazi persecution, which culminated in the ghetto and finally in the death camp, something has been added to the existence of this people: the certainty that anything similar can no longer happen because it must not happen, has imprinted itself on the mind of every Jew, wherever he may be. Only of the Jew? I hope not. The world was traumatized in the most beneficial way by these events, as they were gradually revealed in the course of a quarter-century. Here, too, the Nazi had in the end negated himself: by having brought it about that throughout the world young people, grandchildren of the ghetto contemporaries, still today shout "Gestapo, SS!" when they want to charge repressive powers with vile behavior. The swastika, onto which the Jew had been nailed, not only dispelled the image of the Jewish deicide, but became the universal symbol of what is humanly and historically intolerable. It was the inmates of the ghetto who had paid the price so that humanity could seize the opportunity to deliver itself from evil. *Every* ghetto dweller, mind you, even the black-marketeers, the "collaborators," the cowards, and also the informers. The *highest* price was paid, to be sure, by the most praiseworthy: by the few women and men, in the ghetto or in the extermination camp, who took death into their own hands and, though powerless and unarmed, became avengers.

The history of the ghetto has not ended. It continues, and should continue, to make itself felt. No reconciliation with the murderers who are perhaps still among us, or with the others who, ghostlike, remain before us only as horrid visual memories. That is the highest moral commandment, the only admissible historical mastery of the deeds of the antiman.

There are concepts that have gained an entirely new meaning because of the ghetto. Revenge. Irreconcilability. One must reorient, just as the ghetto dwellers were forced to experience the world in a new way. The Christian ethic is no more adequate for this purpose than the Jewish ethic. A new philosophy of history would have to be written, or rather: it is already in the making. It was the people in the ghetto who recorded its first sentences. Nothing will ever again be the way it once was. Possibly it will be said someday that the history of a more humane humanity began amidst the inhumanity of the ghetto.

Antisemitism on the Left

IT IS NOT A HAPPY moment at which I appear before you to offer my thoughts on the Jewish Problem. It evidently exists once again and, indeed, on an international scale. It's "Brotherhood Week." But where are the brothers? If I were cynical enough, I would quote the American mathematician and chansonnier Tom Lehrer, who already years ago on the occasion of an American "Brotherhood Week" sang: "And the Catholics hate the Protestants and the Protestants hate the Catholics and the Moslems hate the Hindus—and everybody hates the Jews."

Of course, we are still far from a general hatred of the Jews as an ethnic group and religious community; fortunately so, even if we are perhaps not so far from it as optimists assume. Only one thing is already certain: there is a general uneasiness regarding the Jews. One is beginning to feel disturbing reservations, especially among people who only ten years ago tried one's patience with their philosemitic pretenses. Antisemitism has a collective infrastructure that is histori-

"Der ehrbare Antisemitismus," *Merkur* XXX (June 1976): 532–46. This essay was originally delivered as an address ("Respectable Antisemitism") on March 7, 1976, in Hamburg, at the opening session of Brotherhood Week, an interfaith event sponsored annually since 1951 by the *Gesellschaft für Christlich-Jüdische Zusammenarbeit* (Society for Christian-Jewish Cooperation). The English translation first appeared in *Dissent* (Winter 1982).

cally and psychologically deeply imbedded. If it is again becoming a reality today, three decades after the discovery of what was done by the Nazis, then this has to do not only with time, which silently and steadily erodes ethical indignation, but also, indeed probably first and foremost, with the situation in the Near East. It is very dismaying that before our incredulous eyes young people, and particularly those who in the broadest sense of the term regard themselves as socialists, are reviving the age-old phenomenon we had believed was long since dead. We know it from the debate now in progress within the Second International, which traditionally has been well disposed toward the Jews and pro-Israel. The young socialists, to whom the Palestinians now appear as the freedom fighters and the Israelis as the imperialist oppressors, are insisting that the Second International disassociate itself from Israel. For the Third International the question doesn't arise anyway. For it, Israel is an imperialist, cancerous growth and the Jews in general are accomplices of the permanent capitalist conspiracy. The *Führer*, the USSR, commanded and one obeyed.

To be sure, there will be objections that Israel has nothing to do with the Jewish Problem in the broader sense. *One is not antisemitic, but anti-Israel.* It is easy to reply to this objection, all too easy. At this point, please permit me to quote the Germanist Hans Mayer, a man of thorough Marxist schooling. This author writes in his noteworthy book *Aussenseiter (Outsiders)*:

> Whoever attacks Zionism, but by no means wishes to say anything against the Jews, is fooling himself or others. The State of Israel is a Jewish state. Whoever wants to destroy it, openly or through policies that can effect nothing else but such destruction, is practicing the Jew-hatred of yesterday and time immemorial. How clearly this can be observed in the interplay of foreign and domestic politics is shown by the internal policies of the currently anti-Zionist countries. Internally, they will regard their Jewish citizens as virtual "Zionists" and treat them accordingly.

To what extent anti-Zionism makes use of the traditional anti-semitic or anti-Jewish phantasms became clear to me recently while I was reading the French newspaper *Le Monde*, which I do daily. Its special correspondent for the Near East, Michel Tatu, cited a photo volume published by the Egyptian government on the second anniversary of the October War; its text says literally: "In no army of the world are Jews desired . . . because for them money is always more important than principles. . . . Usurers are not fighters." Don't laugh at the fact that this is the voice of a country that in October 1973 was saved in *extremis* by America's pressure on Israel. Rather listen further. The journalist adds that this is a relatively moderate attack, that in the "more hawkish" Arab countries, Syria, Iraq, Algeria, one hears a still quite different tone. There is no need to insist that this sort of thing has nothing in common with—unfortunately "normal"—territorial conflicts between sovereign states such as, for example, the conflict between Algeria and Morocco. It is unadulterated Streicher. It is the most scandalous and, besides, the most stupid antisemitism. But in stating this, we must unfortunately take note of the fact that what is both base and stupid has triumphed more than once in the course of world history, and that there is no relying in the least on Professor Georg Wilhelm Friedrich Hegel.

It is with this outrageous and stupid antisemitism, to the extent that it passes itself off merely as anti-Zionism, that young people are joining forces. Not just a few Nazi offspring of incorrigible parents or grandparents—but alleged socialists. And no one is opposing them with the necessary vigor. On the contrary, the bourgeoisie, whether German, French, or Belgian, breathes a sigh of relief that for once it can march along in the same step with the young generation, which it otherwise regards as a nuisance and whose antiauthoritarian outbursts get on its nerves. Entirely aside from its traditional, dormant antisemitism, this bourgeoisie has its special interests too, which now coincide most exactly and in a comforting way with the thoughtless antisemitism of the young, who often have yet to see a Jew face to face. These bourgeois are interested in business deals: in oil and other things. One must make haste in order to "get in on a good deal," as they put it. *Les affaires sont les affaires.*

Those multinational corporations that in all Western democracies are ready to accede to the Arab boycott demands for the sake of business know this very well. And they are happy at the thought that they, too, for a change, are moving in the direction of the objective spirit—providing that they have ever heard of it. In this way, antisemitism is becoming what it has not been and could not be since the discovery of the Nazi horrors: respectable.

One must concede, to be sure, that antisemitism as such would perhaps not have gained this respectability if there were really not a very deep tie and, if you will excuse the worn-out word, *existential* bond between every Jew and the State of Israel. I say "every Jew," and immediately draw a line; for naturally there are a few self-hating Jews on call everywhere who are prepared to deny this solidarity, which applies to them, too, for the sake of some ideological phantasm or for reasons of both an illusory and a suicidal "objectivity."

Aside from these special cases, who are more to be pitied than censured, the Jews feel bound to the fortunes and misfortunes of Israel, whether they are religious Jews or not, whether they adhere to Zionism or reject it, whether they are newly arrived in their host countries or deeply rooted there. I gladly offer my own person as a not entirely untypical example. I never belonged to the Jewish religious community; I was raised as a Catholic; I have no relatives at all in Israel and soon I will see the country for the first time in my life; I stem from an old Vorarlberg family; my cultural homeland once was Germany; today it is France; for the last thirty-eight years I have been living in Belgium. And yet to the extent that I am interested at all in the national existence and independence of a community, it is Israel.

All this, of course, has nothing to do with any sort of abstruse myths of blood and race. It is very simply that the existence of a Jewish state has taught all the Jews of the world to walk with their head high once more—a Jewish state whose inhabitants are not only merchants but also farmers, not only intellectuals but also professional soldiers, and not those "usurers" that the new Egypt is blathering about, despite all the empirical evidence, but rather, in their majority, craftsmen, industrial and agricultural proletarians. Some Jews had thought that in the socialist societies they would be able to walk upright as a matter of course. The Soviet Union and its vassal countries have done everything imaginable to cure them of their Marxism-Leninism. For this there is no more evident example than the fate of Leopold Trepper, the leader of the spy network "The Red Orchestra,"[1] who had been truly a totally convinced Marxist, and who in the end, driven from his Polish homeland, found refuge in Israel.

When I speak of refuge, I am employing still another key word. For more is at stake for the Jews than just to walk upright. Israel is not only the country in which the Jew no longer permits his enemy to stamp him with a self-image, as Sartre understood it; it is also the virtual shelter for all of the insulted and injured Jews of the earth. Think only of the Jews in the Soviet Union and other Eastern bloc countries, for whom an exit visa to Israel is the last hope of leading a life in dignity and decency. I expressly say: Israel is a *virtual hope*. If these Soviet Jews were to attain full, and no longer insultingly re-stricted, Soviet citizenship, probably only a small percentage of them would want to emigrate to Israel—just as today there are but few American Jews who are pressing into that Mediterranean country de-scribed by Thomas Mann as "dusty and stony." But the virtuality is what counts. If ever somewhere in the world a grim fool should turn up whose *idée fixe* it might be to expel the Jews, the possibility of finding the shelter in Israel that, in Hitler's time—thanks to British Mandate policies—was granted to relatively few Jews, binds every Jew to the fate of this tiny polity in the Near East.

I'd like to see them just once in the face of threat from a new Hitler—Messrs. Maxime Rodinson, Ernest Mandel, Eric Rouleau—all of them Jewish by birth, ideologically alienated, anti-Israel Jews! In lamentable fashion they would haunt the waiting rooms of Israeli consulates in order to secure the piece of paper that would save them, and they wouldn't give a damn about Marx's antisemitic aberrations, which at the moment are still sacred texts to them.

So much for what I have called the existential tie of all Jews to the State of Israel, and this has nothing, absolutely nothing, to do with nationalistic or religious mysticism, which is always only mystification. I am talking about very real, political, social, and psy-chological facts. And already I hear the objections, and the questions: "And the Arabs? And their state? And their national dignity?" They are raised justifiably and demand an answer.

I am no specialist on Middle East questions and no better versed in the history of Zionism than any newspaper reader. But my scant knowledge suffices completely for making a few observations that must be just as obvious to common sense as to those experts who are not ideologically twisted. The Palestinians, who did not exist as a nation when the first Zionist immigrants set foot on the soil of present-day Israel, but who in our time are in the phase of becoming a nation, have a right to a state of their own. The Arabs who inhabited Israeli territory within its borders prior to the Six Day War have a right not to be treated as second-class citizens. I have already said on another occasion that in this entire conflict *right opposes right*.

It must be borne in mind, however, that the rights of the Palestin-ians—those who are now living within the area that became the State of Israel in 1948 and those who were driven from their homesteads by the wars (for which their fellow Arabs, after all, were not so entirely without blame)—the rights of these Palestinian Arabs in principle can be satisfied without insuperable difficulties. What is expected of the one group? That they be loyal citizens of Israel. What is demanded of the others? That once and for all they clearly acknowledge the fact of the Jewish national state. The rest is of a purely technical nature and can therefore be overcome with some intelligence and good will.

And finally, what is expected of a public opinion that, from the far right to the far left, is ready to condemn Israel in the name of national identities and the right to peoples' self-determination? Nothing more than the recognition of the obvious fact that the much-maligned Zionism is also a national liberation movement, that the Jews, too, the most martyred, most tragic people in the world, have a right to their national identity—insofar as they are searching for one and have not already assimilated religiously and ethnically to their host peoples. For that is certainly also a solution, but one that always requires two groups of participants: the ones who are assimilating and the ones who are prepared for their absorption.

All this is terribly banal. But it is nonetheless true since, after all—contrary to a distorted tenet of Adorno's holding that the banal cannot be true—it is always true, for otherwise it could not have become a banality. I repeat: in the Near East conflict *one right opposes another*. And I add: *danger, however, does not oppose danger of the same order*. The fact is that the Arab nations—from the Saudi Arabian despot who is spreading the *Protocols of the Elders of Zion* to the religiously possessed Qaddafi down to the "moderate," pro-Western Sadat and the self-styled Marxist Habash—are all determined to wipe out the State of Israel, as a Herr Göring once wanted to wipe out the cities of England. And it is another incontrovertible fact that in the whole world there is no one who will sound the alarm before a new genocide is set into motion. Really no one? Of course, that isn't entirely true. There are, for example, such personalities as Jean-Paul Sartre and Simone de Beauvoir, known everywhere to be lackeys of imperialism, who protested against the shameless UN and UNESCO decisions. These two and a handful of others. But they have no power. Wherever there is power—from the White House in Washington to the Palais d'Elysée, to Downing Street, or the Kremlin (where they have long ago suppressed the fact that it was mainly Jews who stamped the Motherland of the World's Workers out of the ground of old Russia)—there is the readiness, paraphrasing the matter more or less diplomatically, to defend the "right of the Arabs," which can be quantified in Petrodollars, and to sell the right of the Jews, which is the eternal nonright of the poor, for a few pieces of silver.

This kind of *Realpolitik*—in French one says *"La Réalpolitik"* when speaking of vile opportunism—seeps, uncheckably and constantly, into the lifeblood of what is called public opinion, which, as we know from sociological studies, consists of nothing but opinions about opinions. And we can regard as characteristic of this change in public opinion (not too long ago still favorable to Israel) the behavior of the Christian religious bodies, and especially that of the Vatican. In February 1976, during an Islamic-Christian colloquium—convening, of all places, in Qaddafi's Tripoli—Vatican representatives, first with hesitation but in the end submissively, signed a general condemnation of Israel in which Zionism was once again stigmatized as racism. And in a special reference to Jerusalem it stated: "The Islamic character of Jerusalem is a fact . . . . Judaizing of the city is as much to be avoided as the division and internationalization of the Holy City." One thought one was dreaming: the nightmare of a joint Crescent-and-Cross crusade against Jewry! Surely, the Vatican later disassociated itself from this document that its representatives had, so inconceivably, countersigned. It went even beyond that: at a meeting between Catholic and Jewish theologians in Jerusalem, Rome assumed a position of an almost pro-Israel character.

Nonetheless, the Tripoli colloquium did not vanish from the collective consciousness. Nor does the Vatican's later pro-Israel position disavow what a Moslem participant in Tripoli had assured Western journalists in a private conversation: "The Vatican is isolated," the man had said; "it desperately needs the good will of the Moslem world with its vast population and power."

It actually is the fascination with power that produced this change in the political climate. Nobody wants to swim against the tide, something that everyone knows is quite strenuous. Only few dare to stand by what yesterday was self-evident but now suddenly causes displeasure. Only a while ago it was natural to support the Israelis' right to their sovereignty; and now one suddenly catches oneself feeling that such a declaration has become a real test of courage and that, perhaps, it will become an offense tomorrow. From the political officeholder to the cautious journalist down to the man holding forth on politics on the street corner—everyone looks about expectantly, as though wanting to ask: What and how much is actually permitted again? Whoever has some insight and a bit of flair for recognizing the fluctuations of the forever fluctuating, will be inclined to assure these impatient people that, in fact, a good deal is not only permitted but called for. Wiseacres speak with relief of breaking a taboo, and have no inkling of the dark powers to which they are lending their voices.

The point is, however (and now I return to the subject that I have taken on here), that all this—I mean: the self-alienation of the Left, the interests of international high finance and of the political powers, the maliciousness of the rulers, and the effusive exaltation of the subjected and dispossessed—all this has its effects on the world, in which, today as yesterday, the Jew will be burned. Such is the will of "sound popular instinct" in Harlem (New York), at the regular beer round in some Fürth or another, in the Café de Commerce in Dijon, or in some tiny town in Kent—and, naturally, all the more in every Arab bazaar.

Permit me now to open a parenthesis. In the familiar argumentation of the friends of the Arab cause it is routinely pointed out that in the world of Islam, in contrast to the Christian world, the Jews had always lived together with the Arabs peacefully and by mutual consent. That this was by no means so has been proven most irrefutably in an excellently documented book by Albert Memmi, a Tunisian Jew living in France, a man, moreover, who had always supported the Arabs when they were under French dominion in North Africa.

Antisemitism or anti-Judaism was always a matter of course for the Moslems. In the territory of Islamic rule the Jews were and always remained second-class citizens, and where they worked their way up, as in Moorish Spain, their situation was always precarious. In the most favorable instances they were tolerated, but they were never accepted. That has not changed. While it is possible in Israel for a politician who is a Communist and, at the same time, an Arab nationalist to become the mayor of a city, the few Jews who still live in Syria or Iraq or even in supposedly moderate Tunisia (where they may be no less indigenous than their Arab oppressors) eke out their existence amidst constant humiliation and threat. The Christian world is as little concerned with their fate as with that of the Soviet Jews, for whom not only the road to total assimilation is blocked but also the flight to a land that even under the most difficult economic conditions must appear to them as the "Promised" one.

Existentialist-positivist and stubborn atheist that I am, it doesn't occur to me to convert the Jewish fate into a metaphysical phenomenon. In my eyes the Jews are as little a chosen people as an accursed one. They are nothing but the chance result of historical constellations that were unfavorable to them for two thousand years. Two millennia: that is a very tiny span of time in the unrecordable history of the human species. I can well imagine that a man of the stamp of a Lévi-Strauss, who is occupied with prehistoric societies and their structural myths, smiles gently and a bit scornfully at what are for him such microtemporal courses of events. This member of the Académie Française would cease smiling only if there were a rude knock at his door and a harsh voice, no matter in what language, commanded him, the Jew, to open immediately and come along. To lull himself into a false sense of security would be quite wrong. As we all know, a man of still greater stature—Henri Bergson—was forced to wear the Yellow Star of David before a kind death saved him from the very worst.

No, the Jews and their historical existence are not a metaphysical phenomenon. They are, as I just said, more the victims of chance than of necessity—and also of that *indolence of the heart*, which in the Middle Ages plunged the peasant and in the heyday of capitalism the proletarian into unspeakable misery. Indolence of the heart: I choose to employ this old-fashioned formula. For it summarizes the factual situation better than the most sophisticated sociopsychological studies. The older ones among you may still have witnessed how, in the Third Reich, due to indolence of heart people quickly grew accustomed to their Jewish neighbor being fetched at night and deported.

Today everyone can observe how indolent hearts accommodate themselves when the world everywhere, be it the capitalist or the socialist one, is isolating the Israelis and the Jews who are one with them and thereby abandoning them to the catastrophe that is already hovering over their heads like a storm cloud.

In no time, the Near East question will become a new Jewish question. And we know from history how such a question is answered. The disassociation from Israel and with it from every individual Jew, as cautious as it is clear, hardly surprises the expert on indolent hearts. The millions of Jewish burnt offerings—oh, perhaps there were really "only" five million or even four, and not six million—have been paid off. And now let these eternal troublemakers be quiet; people have other worries; crisis, inflation, unemployment, energy problems. The wretch was led to his fall; suffering will overtake him and, like once Pontius Pilate did, the world will wash its hands of him.

Antisemitism, in the guise of anti-Zionism, has become respectable. I won't elaborate on its roots here. Everyone knows them; enough research has been done on the subject. I will merely state what many newspaper articles, especially in France, have made clear to me. With an indolent heart, people act as if they know nothing of the existential tie of Diaspora Jews to Israel. Obtusely, they do not want to recognize that this union of despair is not whimsical folly, but that it merely expresses the plain fact that the burnt child, the Jew, knows in the depths of his heart where, and where alone, is the aid station willing to tend his burns.

The respectable antisemite has an enviably clear conscience, a spirit as calm as the sea. He also feels in agreement with historical developments, and this is conducive to his moral tranquility. If, occasionally, he awakens from his apathetic drowsing, he asks the ritual questions: Is Israel not an expansionist state, an imperialist outpost? Has not Israel itself caused the trouble that is besetting it from all sides with the "immobility" of its policies? Does not the very idea of Zionism bear in it the original sin of colonialism, so that every Jew who avows solidarity with this land becomes personally guilty? It hardly pays to discuss such questions. After all, Israel's expansion was the result of the bellicose Arab fanaticism that already in 1948 promised the Jews nothing more than to "throw them into the sea." Jewish colonialism was not a colonialism of conquest. The word itself, both etymologically and politically, derives from the Latin *colonus*—farmer. Israel's "immobility" can be explained when we consider the situation of someone who is standing with his back to the wall. This person is not immobile, but a priori immobilized.

All this does not mean that I am unaware of the errors of Israeli policies. But I know, still deeper and more precisely, that Israel's errors are in ridiculous disproportion to the indifference of the others who are motivated entirely by *Realpolitik*, the Russians and the English, the French and the Germans, and tomorrow very likely the Americans—not to speak of the Arabs, who become incomprehensible when at the great feast of their nationhood (which I heartily grant them), they seem compelled to present the Jews as a burnt offering. Human sacrifices without end.

But one is used to such sacrifices, especially when Jews are concerned. The sacrifice of the Jews is in the best tradition, a sanctified custom. One cannot prevail against it. What good then is Brotherhood Week, for which we have gathered here? I admit my pessimism. But since I am not only a born pessimist but by temperament an enlightener, and since, in addition, my home has been situated rather far to the left on the political map my whole life long, I don't wish to shrink from directing a few words to my friends from the leftist camp. The Right would hardly respond to me anyhow. For even where it makes out to be genuinely pro-Israel, it inspires me with skepticism.

Certainly, there is more than one righteous, conservative man—perhaps he is even a former National Socialist—who is earnest about his friendship for the Jews and the State of Israel; and his motivation may have nothing to do with personal relief from guilt but rather with an insight into the facts. This must be expressly stated. Yet, as a mouthpiece of the social class that the Right represents and of the tradition that it upholds and the political heritage that it transmits, it cannot possibly attain that unbiased, humane attitude toward the Jews, which is the only acceptable one. It would be entirely wrong to grant an advance in trust to those circles that a few decades ago were financing Hitler. For them Israel and the Jewish fate are only a welcome argument against everything that dares to question the existing social order. For the Right, let us not forget, stands for order.

But the Jews, and also the Israeli Jews, yes, especially they, are an element of creative disorder. Jews were present wherever fossilized structures were being broken up: in Germany, starting with the "Young Germany" movement to the treatises of the Frankfurt School; in France, as members of the Popular Front, later as disciples of Sartre, and later still as structuralists; in the United States, they are at the center of the liberal movements. And, concerning the Middle East, it was, without a doubt, the Jewish settlers in Palestine, with their attempt to create a democratic socialist society, who awoke the Arab nations from their centuries-long, deep feudal slumber. I ask the Left to consider all this; for although it may have been led astray it is by nature generous. The progeny of Heine and Börne, of Marx and Rosa Luxemburg, of Erich Mühsam and Gustav Landauer cannot, dare not be the ones to spread this respectable antisemitism. For this rabid anti-Zionism will inevitably lead to antisemitism, and for every Jew, no matter where he lives and what political persuasion he adheres to, it is a mortal threat.

I am not exaggerating. With just a bit of imagination everyone can picture what would happen if Israel were destroyed. The surviving Israelis, having once more become mythic Wandering Jews, would flee from the site of the prophet Mohammed and pour out into the world. And again the world would behave as it did after 1933, when such underpopulated countries as Canada and Australia shut their doors to the Jews as though they were bearing germs of pestilence. Again Jews would be forced to earn their living by dubious and illicit work, through obscure financial transactions. For they would not even be acceptable as "guest workers," in times of crisis less than ever before. Once more the public would be concerned with the very old "Jewish Question"—which, if we believe Sartre, never was that but rather always a question of antisemites. No United Nations refugee committee then would be able to invest the Jews with normal civil rights. Anti-Zionism would be dead, all right. But crude antisemitism, aroused from the deepest layers of the collective unconscious and revitalized, would once again create a myth as a result of a historical chance constellation, the myth of the Wandering Jew, of Shylock.

All this, however, would have a twofold result, of which we must urgently be forewarned even now, for time is running out: this twofold result is the total damnation of a human community and also the self-destruction of what yesterday was still the Left. At this very moment, the process is in motion. We are already witnessing how political groups that regard themselves as "leftist" don't waste a word when a despot and paranoid in Uganda commits abominable murders; how they do not protest when the absolute ruler of Libya enacts laws under which adulterous women are stoned; how they are discreetly silent when in Algeria not a single one of the Revolution's great *chefs historiques* any longer appears on the scene. Ben Bella? He merely exchanged the prisons of the French fascist officers for those of the "socialist" Boumedienne. The Left holds its tongue. And to the degree that it talks, its vocabulary is distorted in the truest sense of the word. Stubbornly it terms "progressive" the tyrannic regimes of Syria and Iraq, where occasionally Communists, too, are thrown into jail.

Yet Israel—certainly no model state, but surely a polity that permits opposition, including antinational opposition—is in leftist mythology a "reactionary" land. All this is even worse than those uncanny dialectics that can be used to justify all and everything. It is political hocus-pocus. It is the total confusion of concepts, the definitive loss of moral-political standards.

I believe in all seriousness that the Left must redefine itself within the context of the problem of Israel—that is, the Jewish Problem.

Does the Left still stand up for humanist values? Yes or no? Does it still believe that the concept of democracy embraces universal suffrage, freedom of speech, and the right of assembly—the *droits de l'homme*, which since the French Revolution, after all, have not exactly been unknown? Does the Left still regard nationalism, as it always has, as a political error born of obstinacy? Or, rather, does it find nationalism acceptable wherever, under the sign of tyranny, it is directed against Jews—and unjust as soon as the Jews, for their part and under unbearable pressure, fall reactively into its trap?

Finally: is the Left prepared to acknowledge that even if so-called *formal* democracy cannot attain realization as long as economic democracy does not complement it, that *formal* democracy still must have absolute priority, since economic democracy can be built only on its foundation. Now to the last question: Is the concept of justice still binding for the Left? Justice has been its *raison d'être* as long as it has existed; if the Left sacrifices this concept as a barter for the fetish of revolution, it will destroy itself.

This brings us back to the question of Israel and the Jews. The creation of the State of Israel was an act of justice, as Gromyko, too, clearly proclaimed at the time in the name of the Soviet Union. No one can deny, and I, too, cannot conceal it here that, in carrying out just rehabilitation, injustices toward Arabs have occurred. Nonetheless, the injustice done to the Palestinian Arabs can be redressed without creating a global conflict over the issue. Even today they are not actually homeless, but they possess two states: Jordan, where they constitute the majority of the population, and Lebanon, where in alliance with Syria they are imposing their will. Certainly, it ought to be required that Israel and the Jews of the world contribute their share to the restoration of the full rights of the Palestinian Arabs. But if the Jewish state were destroyed, which is the aim, admitted or not, of all Arab politics from the right to the far left, from the King of Saudi Arabia to George Habash, an *irreversible injustice* would occur. A fleeting glance at history suffices for us to perceive this, if we are at all prepared for objective analyses. Here, precisely at this point, a Left returning to its true self would take up its great task—if it were able to rid itself of a vocabulary to which it is compulsively clinging, and able to rid itself of a few political myths. Were it to withdraw from the Arabs its blind support and mechanical yes-vote, the Left could help solve the problem of Israel, as well as the Jewish Problem.

We can be sure that the great majority of Israeli Jews, who are under such terrible pressure, are willing to seek reconciliation. And we can be sure of the understanding of the Jews outside Israel. The powerful and rich Arab nations need harbor no fears. In a pacified Near East region, the dreamers of a Greater Israel would disappear of their own, just as would the Diaspora Jewry—which is plagued by constant anxiety and thus reacts aggressively. The Left would then have to demand that the Jews be given a double freedom: the freedom to assimilate in their host countries under the aegis of the Enlightenment, and the freedom to emigrate to an Israel that even within the pre-1967 borders would have enough room to receive a flow of immigrants that most likely would not be particularly large.

It seems crucial to me that the Left—which might possibly help to determine the future spirit and image of the Western world—stop pursuing this systematic anti-Zionism, which, for the Jews, and also in historical-objective terms, bears the repulsive features of traditional antisemitism.

Only a few, almost shamefully trivial insights are needed in order to comprehend this. All the young socialists, communists, Maoists, and Trotskyists have to do is imagine those in power telling them: "It isn't you we are combating, it is World Bolshevism. We have nothing against your stand on the Left. However: you are forbidden to be teachers; you are barred from the civil service; your public gatherings will be outlawed; if you continue to form parties you will be overstepping the law." With a minimum of imagination, you need only place yourselves in this situation, and you will understand that with their anti-Zionist emotional fervor these leftists awaken aggressive Zionist reactions on the one hand and, on the other, those antisemitic feelings that have been dragged along through the history of the Occident and the Orient for two millennia and are latently as present today as they ever were. The Left, and with a gesture of sharp rejection, must refuse to allow this antisemitism, now shabbily disguised as anti-Zionism, to become respectable again.

In contrast to a traditionally obstinate Right, the Left has no title to the aforementioned indolence of the heart. It has no title to self-mystification or to an absurd mythology of revolution, no title to that eccentric German idealism that Thomas Mann once characterized by saying, "If it did not sound so presumptuous, one would have to say that the Nazis committed their crimes out of unworldly idealism." If the Left properly understands itself, it knows that it *is a child of the Englightenment*, of the Encyclopedists, the great French Revolution, the intellectual and poetic influence of Lessing, Heine, Börne, Moses Mendelssohn, Feuerbach. It is up to the Left, today more than ever, to concur energetically with Jean-Paul Sartre, who said in an interview in the days of the October War: I know only that in this conflict 3 million people are up against 100 million. In Israel every Jew must be trembling for his life, even if he is the bravest, and with him all of the Jews in every country of the earth.—Perhaps, though, only someone who was a witness to the murderous frenzy of the Third Reich knows and comprehends this.

The person who is speaking to you here *was* a witness. He himself was touched and squeezed, as in the fairy tale of Hänsel and Gretel, not to see whether he was fat enough but, rather, if he was lean enough to be slaughtered. I appeal to your feelings, to the world's feelings, but above all, certainly, to your intelligence, when I stress: antisemitism, even if it calls itself anti-Zionism, is not respectable. On the contrary, it is the indelible stain that mars the honor of civilized humanity.

Please do not regard this appeal as an address to you personally. I know, in any case, that those of you who have gathered here to open Brotherhood Week, no matter where you stand politically, are of sincere good will. Otherwise you would not have come. But since my words have a certain chance of reaching beyond our narrow circle of men and women who are in basic agreement with one another, I chose them as you have heard them. The problem of age-old antisemitism, appearing in the cloak of respectability and fashionable chic, goes far beyond anything that Christian-Jewish cooperation can solve. It is a matter for the world and its history. And wherever and whenever we, who are in agreement, have the possibility, even in the most modest way, to intervene with our word in the historical preceedings that are once again being conducted against the Jews, we are obliged to make ourselves heard: morally, politically, polemically, and with the emotion that befits a good cause.

Eternal Outcasts

Prejudices against Emigrants

IN ALAIN RESNAIS'S last film, *La guerre est finie*, there is a scene that illustrates our theme most vividly: a Scandinavian woman and a Spanish refugee in Paris are stopped in their car because of a minor traffic violation. Now, while the "genuine" foreigner is treated extremely politely by the guardians of order, perhaps because they take her for a tourist, toward the Spaniard, who refers to himself as "refugié espagnol," they show cold and mistrustful rejection. The police don't know who the well-dressed and in every way respectable-looking "refugié" is, how long he has been living in France, what profession he practices, and even whether he may not perhaps hold an important post. The fact alone that he is a *refugee* determines their behavior: prejudice against the emigrant is revealed in its entire petit-bourgeois ugliness and irrational intensity.

If we wish to discuss this kind of prejudice, we will first have to roughly define the concept of the *emigrant*. An emigrant, as we will view him, is defined here in the narrower sense of the word, that is, not only as someone who leaves his country, but as a person who wanted or had to leave his homeland for political, religious, or racial

"Die ewig Unerwünschten: Vorurteile gegen Emigranten," *Tribüne. Zeitschrift zum Verständnis des Judentums* VI (1967): 2230–38.

reasons and who seeks refuge from persecution in a host country. An emigrant in this sense, then, is not the young English engineer who immigrates to the USA because of better work and advancement opportunities, not the Frenchman from Algeria who was repatriated to France after Algeria became independent, not the German from Sudetenland who settled in the Federal Republic; it is the Russian who fled to France after the Bolshevik Revolution, the German Jew who after 1933 attempted to find a new existence in Holland, the Hungarian who in October 1956 crossed over to Austrian territory.

The history of ethnic, political, religious emigration is an essential part of universal history. It begins perhaps with the Jewish Diaspora after the destruction of the Second Temple. It certainly includes the emigrations of the French Huguenots after the recall of the Edict of Nantes, the flight of aristocratic families during the French Revolution, the German and Polish emigrations in the nineteenth century, the already-mentioned Russian flight after the Revolution of 1917, the Italian political emigration after the march on Rome, the drama of the Spanish refugees after the collapse of the republic, the emigration from the Third Reich—down to the exodus in the aftermath of the Second World War and the emigrant air lift from Cuba to the USA. It is not our concern to list all emigrations here; for we are not relating history but are only attempting to elucidate the prejudice against emigrants.

It is obvious that things differ greatly from case to case and that it is not at all easy to generalize. In the countries in which the Huguenot refugees sought asylum, for example, they were received as *coreligionists,* during an epoch when religious denomination meant much more in the common consciousness than nationality. Six hundred Huguenot officers, for instance, were integrated into the army of the prince elector of Brandenburg, in higher ranks than they had held in their own land. Nevertheless, even under these relatively optimal conditions there were hostilities against the immigrants here and there, and in 1694 the French ambassador at the Brandenburg court wrote: "One would think that their religion should make the French refugees well liked; but often [the natives] cannot suffer them and eagerly look for opportunities to cause them ill." The case of the aristocratic refugees from the French Revolution was different still. They did not come into contact with the "people" and scarcely with the "better classes" but rather associated exclusively with other aristocrats, in which situation a bias, provided it existed, tended to be a favorable one. They had, after all, fled from the "canaille," and their hosts behaved toward them as Louis XVI behaved toward his traditional enemy, the English. "With our cousin in St. James," Lion Feuchtwanger had the king say in *Waffen für Amerika*, "we can always come to terms, with the American rebels, never."

And differently structured still was the situation of the German emigrants who fled to the USA after 1848. A good example is Carl Schurz, who had to emigrate because of his participation in the Baden rebellion and who on the other side of the Atlantic became a major general of the Union troops in the American Civil War. For the Americans of that epoch every immigrant of white skin color was a welcome ally in the struggle against the natural environment, which had to be tamed, and an indigenous population not yet entirely subjugated. For a long time the land was to owe its existence and prosperity to immigrants from Europe. Where everyone was a foreigner there were no prerequisites for the development of xenophobia. We do not encounter prejudice against the emigrant until the twentieth century; the frequently cited example of the eternal hatred against Jewish "emigrants" between the destruction of the Second Temple and the emancipation does not count, since animosity toward Jews, until the rise of theoretical, programmatic racial antisemitism in the nineteenth century, was completely religious in nature. The animosity toward emigrants in the twentieth century, then, will have to supply us with the only relevant examples. But first we must stop and ask ourselves a few basic questions.

What is at all special about this particular prejudice? To what extent is it part of the general xenophobic bias? One must proceed with care, and to start with one would do well to differentiate between animosity toward emigrants and prejudice. Certainly in most instances, even if by no means in all, prejudice causes animosity; on the other hand, however, not all animosity toward refugees is based on mere prejudice. The inhabitants of those countries that were struck by the great economic crisis of the years 1930–39 and in which the refugees from Hitler sought asylum, had very real economic reasons to fear the competition of the emigrants in the job market. Their animosity toward them, therefore, can in no way be explained solely on the grounds of prejudice. But in this regard, too, there is always a very ambiguous situation; for even when work of any kind was forbidden to the refugees (in Belgium and Holland, for example), animosity made itself felt. It had two aspects; it was both real worry about subsistence (for, after all, there always was the possibility of illicit work and thus competition from the refugee), and pent-up, irrational fear. The emigrant appeared as a *stranger*, to whom one ascribed magic powers in the struggle for life solely because of his strangeness, which simply means that a *pre-judgment* was passed on him. That provides the answer to the question posed above, and we come to the conclusion that prejudice against the emigrant is a *special case of more general xenophobic prejudice*. On the latter much work has been done by social psychologists, so that we believe we are spared an elucidation of prejudice using psychological methods. But let us attempt to sketch the outlines of a phenomenological interpretation of xenophobia.

The alien, we would think, is the unfamiliar and therefore by definition also threatening. A human being inhabits a world, an area where the same language is spoken, a specific civilization, a landscape. He internalizes this world and it forms part of his personality. Where a foreign, unfamiliar world, that is to say, a foreign language, civilization, and foreign patterns of behavior collide with him, he feels threatened and injured to the core of his being. The stranger, the strangeness invade not only his landscape and his linguistic domain but also the deepest strata of his person. Until then he had regarded his person as a self-contained, invulnerable unit, a monad without windows; his cultural and linguistic environment was for him the world absolute. Suddenly, through the intrusion of the alien, he is made to realize that his inner unity can be destroyed and that his country, since it apparently is not the entire world, offers him no protection. The person who encounters strangeness in his own country feels approximately like an exile in a foreign land. To the uninvited guest his values mean nothing and his words have only partial meaning. He answers to what he believes is threatening him and what now really has disturbed his equilibrium with a resistance that can reach the point of hatred. For this to happen only a very vague experience is necessary; the threat alone suffices. The judgment on the stranger is conditioned by the prejudice against him; he needs only to knock at our door and already we assume a defensive position.

It is obvious that the xenophobic prejudice originating in this manner is most intense among what Friedrich Heer calls the "lower folk." The educated social classes, versed in languages and with knowledge of foreign countries, are more immune to it. For this reason, as paradoxical as it may seem at a first fleeting glance, animosity toward foreigners as a general phenomenon is perhaps not as much tied to the rise of nationalism as to democracy. In times during which the common people did not enter the picture, so to speak, the foreigner as gentleman and educated person was a guest only of a gentleman and an educated person, and the common man was expected only to bow and show respect. For the gentleman and educated person, in turn, the stranger was by no means the alien in the sense alluded to earlier. The world of the guest was not a strange, uncanny one but rather the host's own. The Frenchman René Descartes was surely closer to Queen Christine of Sweden than any of her peasant subjects. From all this it becomes clear that scarcely any xenophobic prejudice against emigrants was shown toward the Huguenot refugees and none at all toward the refugees from the 1789 Revolution; whereas in the twentieth century of democratic mass society it emerged with concentrated aggressiveness.

We felt justified in attributing the prejudice against emigrants to some basic facts of xenophobia. But the former is a special case of the latter and does not entirely coincide with it. It is precisely because of its special nature that it interests us; but this special nature, again, has the most varied ramifications, so that it is most difficult to find distinct guidelines. The prejudice against the refugees from the Russian Revolution, every one of whom in Paris claimed to be an ex–grand duke and who in many instances did in fact arrive in the country with a fortune, was different from the prejudice directed against the poor Spaniards who in 1939 hiked across the Pyrenees with rolled-up woolen blankets. The prejudice against the Jewish emigrant from Hitler was more deeply rooted and more aggressive than the resistance that refugees from the communist countries after the Second World War had to overcome. In the prejudice of the inhabitants of Florida against Cuban emigrants racist elements can be ascertained; in the rejection of the non-Jewish German emigrants from the Third Reich, economic fears were primarily decisive. Where can one find the starting point for an analysis that will lead to general conclusions?

The following facts appear undeniable: For the population of the host country the emigrant is a person who was chased from his own land, and even today no one in the broad democratic masses—which are perhaps manipulated, but in the last analysis really are the sovereign bearers of public opinion—can really quite imagine that someone had to leave his country without fault. In each citizen, no matter how enlightened he may be, there is an irrational respect for the authorities, his own as well as someone else's. The authorities cannot really be wrong (so thinks or feels the inhabitant of the host country, without actually articulating the thought). The emigrant, then, must have "done something" if he crossed the border on smugglers' routes by night and fog without a passport. His external appearance alone arouses mostly vague notions of delinquency or at any rate personal neglect. He is poorly dressed and is inclined to band together with his own, which to the eye appears like a conspiracy. The resident citizen, "bien de chez soi," thinks at the sight of him: No doubt they knew what they were doing when they threw him out.

In addition there is a mistrust that has its roots in even deeper strata. The alien, we said, is by definition the unfamiliar. It becomes doubly suspect when it is indeterminable in its alien nature. Here is a Hungarian. Fine. He speaks the language of his host country with a strong accent, differs from the people among whom he seeks asylum by his physiognomy, bearing, gestures. He is the stranger. But what kind of stranger? Is he at least a "real" Hungarian, like the one we met last year perhaps, on a summer trip to Lake Balaton? Quite obviously not. After all, he wants as little to do with his fatherland as it wants to do with him. Perhaps he is inclined to an overly hasty, all too eager readiness to assimilate—which, however, by no means makes him appear more familiar and more dependable to those who are to assimilate him. Thus, in the end he becomes doubly alien: in his quality as a foreigner and in his national indefinability.

Certainly, the degree of prejudice that becomes animosity is to a large extent dependent on the consensus or on the conformism prevailing at a given time in the host country. There is no doubt that all those emigrants who during the period of the Cold War fled from communist countries to the West received a friendlier welcome than once did the antifascist refugees from Hitler, and not only by the authorities. For public opinion, brought into conformity by the press, radio, and other mass media, an emigrant who came from Czechoslovakia to Belgium in 1950 was, to be sure, still an "alien" in the previously defined sense, but the mistrust was eased by the fact that one saw in him a human being who had fled from radical evil, i.e., communism. The press spoke of him as someone who had "chosen freedom." That certainly did not make the deep-rooted prejudice disappear, but it did dilute it considerably. Of course, one must realize that because of the prejudice against everything communist, this diluting or neutralization of the prejudice against emigrants was mostly superficial and therefore of short duration. If today a metal worker in France, Belgium, Holland, etc., who fled from Hungary in 1956, commits a burglary, one can be sure that the newspapers will not report about the "metal worker Bela Horvath" who in a cigar store appropriated the day's receipts but rather about the "Hungarian refugee Bela Horvath," even if the person in question has long since become naturalized.

Of course, the situation of the emigrant is worst by far wherever several prejudices accumulate against him. Once again one must speak here of the antifascist emigrants from Hitler, who, according to our firm conviction based on years of personal experience, suffered under prejudice in the most tragic way.

The emigrant from Hitler was a refugee. In addition, in the great majority of cases he was a Jew. And politically he often stood on the far left. Inevitably, the general hostility against emigrants and the antisemitic and anticommunist prejudice consolidated in an outright monstrous manner into a compact bloc. Hermann Kesten, probably the best authority on the emigration after 1933, wrote in a book he edited, *Ich lebe nicht in der Bundesrepublik:*

> Many exiles came without a passport and were locked up because of that. . . . Because they had illegally crossed, let us say, the French border, they were locked up by the French police without a hearing and after their release they were chased across the Belgian border. Caught by the Belgians, they were incarcerated—with, or without, a hearing; after serving their term they were chased at night, illegally, across the border and locked up by the French anew, now for a longer term because of repeated illegal border crossings; after that they were once again chased to Belgium, say, again imprisoned by the Belgians under more severe terms, thereafter chased across the border, ad infinitum; and perhaps the victims would still be rotting today in who knows what border jails if they had not long since been murdered in Dachau or gassed in Auschwitz by their more radical countrymen. In most countries the exiles were not allowed to work, but they were also not allowed to be without any means of subsistence. They were not permitted to be politically active, perhaps in order not to disturb the political agitation of the National Socialists abroad.

At this point one should go on—something Kesten unfortunately omitted to do—and analyze more precisely the antisemitic conformism, hostile likewise to emigrants and the Left, that in the end combined with the desire for peaceful coexistence with Germany. If we survey the history of emigration in this century, we will soon realize that the liberal and, in the broadest sense, leftist emigrant has consistently had it more difficult than his rightist-oriented companion in misfortune. Because in the West power—once again, in the broadest sense—was everywhere the power of the Right, the conformism hostile to the emigrants was also rightist oriented. The vexations and insults that the Italian, Spanish, and German antifascist refugees had to put up with from the government agencies and the population of their host countries (since they were regarded as a danger for the existing order) were more numerous and offensive than those to which the Russian refugees from the Revolution after 1917 and Polish, Hungarian, and Czech emigrants in the 1950s were exposed. And if in addition there was antisemitic prejudice, the situation of the exile psychologically became absolutely unbearable.

The understandable, more or less pronounced desire for coexistence with just that country that sent or sends emigrants, plays a significant role in the formation of prejudice hostile to them. It would be senseless not to admit that political emigrants are "bellicose" as long as they have even the slightest hope that their fatherland can be freed by war from the regime they hate and that hates them. The French revolutionary emigrants, ex-minister Charles A. Calonne and general Marquis de Bouille, were on the side of the Prussians and participated in the battle of Valmy. The Russian emigrants of 1917 founded in Paris a center for anticommunist activism (under Savinkov, at one time Kerensky's war minister, who later entered the Soviet Union illegally and was executed there). At first they concentrated their hopes on the interventionary campaigns by the Western powers, finally on the great antibolshevik war, which then actually was unleashed by Hitler. The emigrants from Hitler, particularly among their politically conscious segments, were likewise *for* the war. And occasionally they produced most unfortunate results, as did, for example, Leopold Schwarzschild with his weekly *Das neue Tagebuch*, in which prior to the war one could read every week that Hitler's Germany was economically on the verge of ruin, that the German tanks and planes were worthless, that the war would be a military walkover. The numerous "national committees" of refugees from the communist-ruled countries of the Eastern bloc behaved quite similarly after the Second World War. There were moments in the peak days of the Cold War when in these circles ministerial posts were being assigned for the Hungary, Poland, Lithuania, etc., that were to arise after the Third World War. And does anyone need to be reminded of the activities of the Cuban refugees in Florida?

The attitude of the emigrants is understandable. It is just as understandable that, starting with the emigrants from the Russian Revolution to the Cuban refugees, they are regarded only as pawns in the game of power politics. Characteristic of this tendency is the behavior of the USA toward the Gaullist-French emigrants during World War II, who were haughtily ignored as long as one wanted to maintain good relations with Vichy, and who were allowed to enter the scene of world politics only when, thanks to de Gaulle's extremely skillful maneuvering and stubbornness, the internal and external resistance of Gaulist forces became a real political power.

Political emigrants are bellicose as long as they can reasonably entertain hopes that the regime hostile to them will be overthrown and they will be able to return home. As a judgment based on experience and, in turn, as a prejudice this position has negative consequences for them only when the people as a whole have a political say. The revolutionary emigrants of 1789 could push for war as much as they wanted; the people, whose sole duty was to obey and provide soldiers anyhow, did not take a position either in their favor or against them. After the collapse of France in June 1940, on the other hand, Petain's government, already dependent on the approval of the population and for this reason democratically conditioned despite its dictatorial character, found it easy to present the lost war as the work of the emigrants from Hitler—who had indeed desired it but had contributed exceedingly little to its outbreak. Once the people become an active factor in political events, the host country's wish for coexistence with the homeland that expelled the emigrant becomes crucial for him. Between 1933 and 1939 the world wished to coexist with Hitler; that is why animosity toward the "subversive," "warmongering" emigrant was a dominant collective feeling in almost all countries. In the 1950s the attitude toward coexistence with communism was different. In the West people thought that the Third World War was already in sight; the emigrants appeared as potential allies and therefore their fate became somewhat bearable. However, it must be emphasized once more that even under such optimal conditions the situation of the emigrant in the host country and among the host people is a precarious one. With time it will inevitably become calamitous. If the desire for coexistence arises (as it has today in most Western countries), the emigrant, who for existential reasons opposes the change of situation and constantly calls for vigilance and mistrust of his former homeland, generally loses sympathy. But even if the idea of coexistence totally collapses and war breaks out and the emigrant is no longer a potential but rather a factual, arms-bearing ally, reservations toward him remain. The fate of the Gaullists in London provides the most striking example: between 1940 and 1945 they were England's allies, but despite that they were not much liked by the English.

In discussing the animosity toward the emigrant arising from political considerations and fears that are very real even though they are by no means always justified, we have seemingly digressed from our topic. But only seemingly. For in the end it turns out that the intended conceptual differentiation between animosity (which can have reasonable causes) and prejudice (which is always irrational) is an impossible abstraction. Namely, there exists a dialectical relation between judgment based on experience and prejudice, between "judgment" and "prejugé." A prejudice that is not based on at least some sort of genuine insight can hardly ever be proven. In order for the host people to have prejudices against emigrants it must know emigrants, if only slightly or even through hearsay. In reality, the judgment based on experience (once again, a vague experience) and prejudice cannot be kept apart so easily as in theoretical reflection. They originate together in an interaction that in certain circumstances assumes the character of a *circulus vitiosus*. The emigrant comes penniless to the host country, unable to speak its language, unfamiliar with the working conditions there, and appears on the street, in the restaurants and railway stations, etc. not only as an alien but also as an idle and neglected element. An unclear "judgment based on experience" is passed on him, and it says that emigrants are dirty, reluctant to work, and not ready to assimilate. This vague and uncertain experiential judgment hardens into prejudice and the latter now retroacts upon every new experiential judgment. In the end such dynamics place the emigrants in situations in which they actually do resemble the prejudicial caricature that has already penetrated the collective consciousness.

Someone who gets no work because he is a foreigner, in the end becomes unaccustomed to work; someone who does not get an apartment in a decent residential area because "foreigners" are "not wanted" there, ends up living in the filth of the slums; he whom the host people do not want to assimilate, with the bit of pride still remaining him, will finally not want to hear anything of assimilation; together with his countrymen and comrades in fate, he will remain an eternal alien element in the host country. No matter what he does, it is wrong. If he shows restraint in order not to become conspicuous, he is only an incompetent idler; if he shows ambition and diligence, he is an unbearable careerist. If he seeks personal contact with the host people, he is ingratiating himself; if he sticks to his own kind, he is despised as being unadaptable.

In the end, it is always his not precisely definable *strangeness* that makes him appear suspect. The foreign worker in his cheap suit at the railway station may meet with hostility because of his strangeness and poverty (which for the dominant religion of success is always a disgrace); he nevertheless remains an Italian, a Greek, a Turk. A ray of prestige from his own country, no matter how poor, indeed underdeveloped, it may be, falls upon him too. The *emigrant*, however, even if he is naturalized, even if he has achieved a fairly respectable social position, remains an unknown in a calculation that never works out.

The Time of Rehabilitation
The Third Reich and Historical Objectivity

SOMETIMES TRIFLES are enough to suddenly cause the "scales to fall from one's eyes," as the saying goes—plain bagatelles, simple little somethings, which, however, precisely because of their simplicity, illuminate the scenery of an epoch like flares.

Thus, in a prestigious Swiss weekly, a well-meaning liberal-conservative paper that doesn't hesitate now and then to grant me space for modest commentaries, although I am considered to be on the left, I recently read a review of the French film *Le vieux fusil*. The film, certainly no masterpiece of its category but still a suspenseful political thriller, had as its subject the story of an unpolitical surgeon who, during the time of France's occupation by the Nazis, also treats wounded Maquis men and shelters them in his hospital. As a result, the SS together with French collaborators gruesomely cause the doctor's young wife and little daughter to burn to death, in an operation like that of Oradour. The deeply wounded man suddenly feels himself torn out of his middle-class value system and plunged into a jungle of resistance, aggression, injured honor, and thirst for revenge. Instincts

"Die Zeit der Rehabilitation: Das Dritte Reich und die geschichtliche Objektivität," in *Österreichische Autoren bei Klett-Cotta* (Austrian authors published by Klett-Cotta), ed. Kurt Biak and Michael Klett (Wien: ÖBV-Klett-Cotta Verlagsgesellschaft m.b.H., 1981), pp. 21–35.

are laid bare in him that he would never have dreamed of in normal circumstances. In a tragic frenzy of retribution, he methodically kills one after another of the SS murderers with an old hunting rifle.

To repeat, the film was no masterwork. But quite aside from the tour de force of the main actor, Philippe Noiret, it did faithfully convey a slice of reality in France in the year 1944. From the cinematic point of view, the critic certainly could have justifiably objected to this or that aspect of the film. But he decided not to. Instead, he gave free rein to his irritation, claiming that the film was "political propaganda." The historical facts didn't concern him much. He obviously found it outrageous that the SS was portrayed as being what it was: blue-eyed, battle-hardened, vile, pitiless—and stupid to boot. He found this stereotyped, outmoded, and worn-out, and didn't take the trouble to investigate whether the Death's Head units of the Third Reich had not, in fact, behaved exactly as the cliché claims—in which case, of course, it would no longer be a cliché but an objective statement, as banal and true as the assertion "Snow is white."

I read that and suddenly understood what had already been in the making for a few years, but to which I had closed my eyes: that the *time of rehabilitation* had dawned. It seems that they finally wanted to approach the Third Reich, which became a myth since from the very start it was meant to become a myth, with "historical objectivity." The prelude was probably Joachim Fest's Hitler best-seller, a cleverly gotten-up biography of the Emil-Ludwig or Stefan-Zweig sort, in which a Hitler was presented to us "from the human angle." Having said this, I must immediately note that the phenomenon of rehabilitation is not a specifically German but rather an international trend; if you wish, it is a "change of tenor." In just a moment we will discuss to what extent the pendulum swing is taking place abroad.

First, however, it is necessary to treat the question of whether "historical objectivity" should, or can, exist at all, and particularly in this case. It is certainly true that moral indignation cannot hold its ground against the silently erosive and transformative effects of time. It is hopeless, even if not entirely unjustified, to demand that National Socialism be felt as an outrage with the same emotional intensity as in the years immediately following the Second World War. No doubt, there exists something like historical entropy: the historical "heat gradient" disappears; the result is a balance with no order. But in viewing historical processes we should not foster this entropy; on the contrary, we should resist it with all our power, if only for the reason that even distribution of the historical molecules would no longer permit us to discern a coherent picture of history. More decisive for humane concerns, however, is the demand that the study of history contain a component of *moral judgment*, as do the historical events themselves. Reality is reasonable only so long as it is moral. And as a concern of humanity, historicity becomes *unnatural* as soon as it pretends to be neutral to values. Seen in this way, the myth of the Third Reich as a myth of radical evil is truer to fact than an alleged objectivity that does not oppose the evil and already by its indifference alone becomes the advocate of this very evil.

In regard to our problem, the Germans—as previously indicated—are less to be reproached than their former enemies within the western alliance. The Germans are about to establish themselves politically as the world power that economically they have already been for a long time. They have no need at all to initiate reparations proceedings for the benefit of the Nazis. They can generously confine themselves to making a celebrity of their Speer and, for the rest, to say that the others were really not that much better, and now they're admitting it themselves. Since the "Gulag Archipelago" it appears more and more probable, they say, that Hitler was the wrong swine to be slaughtered, and what about the atrocities of Vietnam, and Watergate, and Lockheed! Just take a look at all that, and what do people want of us Germans? And why all the needless uproar about the Third Reich?

No doubt whatsoever, *France* is their best ally. In this country, the Résistance was already an annoyance for President Pompidou: "La résistance m'agace," the man said. No doubt, the sinister Petain will soon have his grave of honor in Verdun. They are constantly at pains there, for reasons of "historical objectivity," and because veterans, as is well known, are infamously ridiculous, to assure the mighty neighbor to the east that they are not rancorous; rather they are resolved to stir up so much dust in front of their own door that one can no longer discern the facts of the past. In so doing, this nation (which does not tire of celebrating Ernst Jünger, while it sovereignly ignores Heinrich Mann) is losing all political, moral, and esthetic standards. Despite Belgian protests, in France the collaborator-writer Félicien Marceau, who was sentenced to prison *in contumaciam* in Brussels, gets elected to the Académie Française. Thanks to the novel *The Ogre*, solemnly tedious and suffocating in the Masurian swamp of its own utterly false lyricism, the Germanist Michel Turnier became the quasi-official interpreter of the German soul in France. He, and not Robert Minder or Pierre Bertaux! At approximately the same time, the cleaning-up at home began. Ferdinand Céline, with his paranoid verbal mishmash, was rediscovered and restored to his rights, an author who certainly borders on genius but constantly crosses its borders into the realm of insanity. For reasons of tact, one no longer speaks of his book *Bagatelle pour un massacre*, which literally urges a general pogrom. The Blood-and-Soil poet Jean Giono, an equivocal "pacifist" and staunch proponent of the Munich Agreement, was, and is, pampered so heartily that in all seriousness a "Society of the Friends of Giono" is making efforts to have his house in Provence classified as a historical monument.

The worst things went on in the cinema. The turning point was reached in the zeal for objectivity shown by the producers of the documentary television film *Le chagrin et la pitié*, which revealed nothing other than the truly not original fact that the heroes are growing weary, the old feeble-minded, and that not all Frenchmen participated in the epic adventure of resistance. It gave the French the good conscience of objectivity and the Germans the assurance that, when it was all or nothing, the others were not that much better than they. A signal for departure to new shores. It didn't take long for the talented Louis Malle to present us with his *Lacombe, Lucien* (a good film, definitely better than *Le vieux fusil*), which, to be sure, boiled down to nothing else but a clever defense of collaboration and Nazi torture. Lucien Lacombe was just a poor devil; as such he slipped into fascist criminality—from which one could conclude with dead certainty that, seen by the light of day, all Nazi murderers, including Himmler, were poor devils. Tout comprendre, c'est tout pardonner. So they pardoned (like the dear Lord, whose metier is pardoning), and thus also threw open a back door that was wide enough to let bestiality in again.

Even more shameless, thanks to its commercially clever injection of the sadomasochistic trend into the move toward rehabilitation, was the film *The Night Porter* by the Italian director Liliana Cavini. Here the peak of narrative foolishness and moral reprehensibility is attained. The masochistic fling of a former deportee, who finds one of her past torturers in the figure of a night porter and discovers that the trick with the chains and the whips and the blood is actually not without a certain charm, was sold to a crowd oscillating between insensitivity and snobbism. To top it off, the aggravating person responsible for the scandalous film even had the gall, in an interview she granted to a French weekly, to support her notions by referring to Freud and Nietzsche. All the just indignation of those who had once been directly affected by the adversity was to no avail. The Sade-Bataille chic of the pseudo-intellectuals celebrated repulsive triumphs. Together, games and twaddle appropriated the enormities and prospered. Weary of it all, one would like to bow out and tell oneself that these people are stupid and full up to the gills with undigested blather. The best thing is to turn one's head to the wall and forget it.

This is not permissible, however. Not yet. Time has not yet completed its work of effacing the differences; that is to say, the social "heat gradient" caused by the Nazi crimes has not yet been equalized by historical entropy. Protest is absolutely necessary if a historical picture is not to be falsified, a picture in whose features we recognize the radical evil that cannot be compared with any earlier occurrences and, I am convinced, will not be matched in heinousness by anything that may yet come. It didn't matter much that the intelligent Susan Sontag protested against the modish, international idolization of Leni Riefenstahl and her inflated kitsch (that harmonized so well with the plaster pylons of Herr Speer and to which the ultra–avant-garde *Cahiers de Cinéma* is kowtowing). From the USA I received the news that Veit Harlan's anti-Czech propaganda film *Die goldene Stadt* (i.e., Prague) is being shown there with great success in movie houses intended especially for German-language programs. And when, gentlemen, will *Jud Süss* finally return to favor? The film is not really that irrelevant at a time when a new antisemitism ventures forth in the guise of "leftist" anti-Zionism. The disputants, who become enraptured at the deeds of North and Black African despots, are closing the circle in the direction of the philistine beer-table regulars for whose adversaries they mistake themselves, whereas in truth they are their complement.

The perverse copulation of the Right and Left that reveals itself to us in the rehabilitation wave goes deeper and is more uncanny than rightist and leftist debaters suspect. Susan Sontag's clear recognition that the fuss about Leni Riefenstahl is at least partly traceable to agitation by the feminist "Left" hits upon *a* truth but not the entire truth. The latter is so complicated that in the space at my disposal I must make do with indications. Therefore, just this much: Behind the utterly false fascist esthetics that finds "beauty" not only in a film of a Reich's party rally but, if need be, in scenes of political torture, there hides bad old irrationalism in very modern get-up. It assumes the most varied and, I won't deny it, at times most attractive forms. It can appear as Spengler transformed into Michel Foucault. As the Wilhelm-Reich cult, it can spurn Freud's civilized "sublimation" and profess a sexual excess at whose logically predictable end there is not "sexual pleasure" but violence and murder. It can drape itself structuralistically as a Rousseau renascence and thus abandon humanism. (I suggest as a therapy Lévy-Bruhl's book *Primitive Mentality*.) Irrationalism, which is one of the breeding grounds for the rampant spread of the rehabilitation weed, appears in one place in the form of the "anti-Oedipus" of Deleuze and Guattari, who are working on an anarchistic anthropology; it appears elsewhere clothed in the communist-Catholic priest's robe of a Roger Geraudy, who prostrates himself before primitive social communities and simultaneously knocks at the door of the Catholic hierarchy, all the while insisting on his Marxism; still elsewhere it turns up in the obtrusive promotion of regional folkloristic group games that need only to be called "identity-finding," rather than custom and usage, in order to make them respectable.

That all this did not descend on us like a bolt from the blue is clear. *Raison* deteriorated to capitalistic-technocratic *ratio*, and compromised itself so much through the practices it served that every mental effort shrinks back before it like a horse rearing up in fright. No "Critical Theory" helped. There was no longer salvation in neo-Marxism. On the contrary, now the "Dialectics of Enlightenment" became an obvious danger. Historical objectivity, it was decreed, demands that the seed of fascism be seen already in the Enlightenment, that the latter be regarded as "having failed" (not: as "having been overpowered"!) and that the former be analyzed with an "objectivity" that is beyond all ethics as a state of consciousness of the *Weltgeist*.

In the end, the German philistine's magic horn poured out the same gifts as that highbred intellectuality in Paris and New York whose sole link with intelligence is purely etymological. The nonsense that after Auschwitz a poem was no longer possible quickly became the assurance that twaddle was not only possible but indispensable: at the regular beer-round and in the seminar. Historicity turned into historical indifference and thereby renounced itself. It is no accident that Lévi-Strauss is a rabid Wagnerian, like the Thomas Mann of

Reflections of a Nonpolitical Man. No, even worse: like those Teuto-maniacs cloddishly stumbling along in the tracks of H. S. Chamber-lain. In the process of rehabilitation the circle closes vexatiously not only from Right to Left, but also from the superacuminous to the plain imbecilic. Intellect and cultivation are the orphans. And let no one be surprised if a German nationalism that never before felt so good as in the days when it caused the rickety bones of civilization to tremble, boldly rears its abominable head. It has nothing to fear since the intellectual Left relinquished its arms and has been reveling in a mis-understood Rousseauism and Nietzscheanism, which it combined, in a self-delusory sleight-of-hand, with a Marx whose ethical-prophetic élan is rigorously denied for the sake of Althusser's sanctity of the "text." And Freud's pessimistic humanism of sublimation was hushed up in favor of Lacan's value-neutral "structured discourse." What Ju-lien Benda called in his day "la trahison des clercs" is coming to pass in the general rehabilitation of barbarism—which one hardly dares to designate as such anymore, so great is the fear that one could be dismissed as a "veteran" by a Right that no longer feels morally bur-dened and a Left that fervently throws itself at every current fashion.

Well, of course: veterans are comical when they hold their pitiable ceremonies, which are becoming shabbier from year to year. They are dead serious when, as the old generation, full of lived history and assimilated historicity, they raise their warning voices, in the awareness that their actions are futile. Only long after they are gone will it turn out that as the untimely ones of their day they were more in step with the times than the others who are blindly dashing into a future that they themselves are blocking without knowing it. As for me, I don't have the slightest illusions. Rehabilitation, once begun, counter to morality and history, will take its course. In England they will discover that Oswald Mosley was not such a fool after all. In France, where already at the present hour the worst murderers, am-nestied, are enjoying a peaceful old age, official opinion gone astray will weigh Pétain and Laval into a pseudohistorical equilibrium pro-duced with the help of false weights. And Germany? Well, that is clear: since all the preliminary categorizations have been taken care of, it will no longer wish to deny Hitler his place in the Feldherrenhalle. There will be some difficulties only in the case of the Invalides: the corpus delicti cannot be located. Historical objectivity, so they say, always operates beyond good and evil, and they indiscriminately file evil away, whereby good, too, disappears from the agenda. Dialectics contributed generously to an undertaking that is self-righteously represented as "demystification," whereas in truth it is merely fostering a new and more dangerous mystification. Bourgeois morality was justifiably rejected as ideology, but in the process, morality pure and simple—which also wore bourgeois dress—went to the dogs along with it. No one seems able to recognize that in certain historical constellations subjective outrage accords exactly with humane reality.

As Ernst Bloch put it, one need not at all have a precise idea of the humane in order to recognize beyond any doubt that Nero was a monster. In our context this statement can be reformulated to mean that the myth of evil embodied by the Third Reich has more objective character than does dialectical demystification. Thomas Mann's biblical maledictions ("What right do you actually have still to be alive?") possess greater value, not only morally but also politically, than a self-alienated intelligentsia's historical constructions that, in the name of a falsely conceived objectivity, boil down to rehabilitation.

But the way things are there is little prospect that this will be comprehended. The old Brown Shirts have every imaginable chance to give the few remaining simpletons with their talk of repentance one more whack on the skull. And the New Reds will be unable to protest. For what is sauce for Qaddafi must also be sauce for the Führer. Only more so.

Wasted Words

Thoughts on Germany since 1945

ANGER KEEPS ONE YOUNG, they say. But if it is accompanied by a feeling of complete impotence, it leads to a mournfulness that is not a "work of mourning" in the psychoanalytic sense but resignation. And resignation ages one, no doubt about it. Speaking out is a waste of words. The voice grows brittle, must fade and die even before the speaker exits. Nonetheless, the impotent anger is there. Its causes, and also the effects that are still possible despite all, will be my subject here. Therefore, I will begin by asking permission to speak in the first person. For there is a degree of personal involvement that turns every attempt at detachment into not only a psychological falsification but a moral and political one as well. How were things then and how are they now?

In 1945, "arisen from the dead" (to borrow a phrase from the Catholic Creed), my head still heavy from the blows and my own useless brooding, I imagined that the world belonged to us, the defeated who had become victors, the utopians whose most extravagant dreams suddenly appeared to be surpassed by reality, the visionaries

"In den Wind gesprochen," in *Die zornigen alten Männer: Gedanken über Deutschland seit 1945* (The angry old men: thoughts on Germany since 1945), ed. Axel Eggebrecht (Reinbek bei Hamburg: Rowohlt Verlag, 1979), pp. 258–79.

of a future that was now the present and that today seems even to us as the most distant past. Radical evil, so we thought, was destroyed. One had only to set about clearing away the filth that it had left behind and the world would be as we had wished it: free, just, and fraternal. How naïve, indeed, how childish must our ideas have seemed to our contemporaries, especially the young ones! How naïve were we, in fact? Exactly as naïve as anyone else who believes that hope can ever be completely realized.

As for me, after my liberation in 1945 from two years of concentration camp imprisonment, I was completely unable, and probably also not at all willing, to recognize, to perceive the real power relations: who was now against whom and would be tomorrow. While entirely new fronts were already forming and many believed, in keeping with a pronouncement attributed to Winston Churchill (rightly or wrongly, I don't know), that in Hitler one had "slaughtered the wrong pig," we were still living within the mentality of the Résistance. Whoever had fought against Hitler was our friend; whoever had been on the side of the monster was our enemy. That's how simple everything seemed to us. Americans, Englishmen, Frenchmen, Russians, liberals, militant Catholics and Protestants, socialists, communists: they were all equally welcome as our comrades. For us the USA was still Roosevelt and his New Deal and the Soviet Union was the land of the great sacrifice, thus holy and irreproachable. If someone told us of the bitter fights that had been fought, still during the war, between the right and left wings of the resistance movements, we stopped our ears. Before our eyes, the "last battle" was being fought in France between de Gaulle and the communists, in which both were losers. But we did not want to see it. There was only Nazism and anti-Nazism. (As yet no one on the Left was slyly concealing the concept of Nazism behind that of "fascism," nor on the Right behind that of "totalitarianism"). We lived in the illusion of a "Popular Front" that embraced all of the democratic forces, from a bourgeois but upright Babbitt to an Ivan Ivanovitch who was zealously attending the ideology courses of the Communist Party.

We were, I hope, not stupid. But we were miserably informed— and besides that, my skull ached. Also, we were not free of a victory euphoria that no doubt appears comical today. Perhaps we had done nothing more than distribute flyers that were as foolishly conceived as they were ineffective. But this, so we believed, gave us the right to march in rank and file with the defenders of Stalingrad and the British and American soldiers who had landed in Normandy. Today *we* may laugh at such nonsense; but I forbid even the faintest smirk to those who were not with us in the abyss, be it that they were too young, be it that they were too cautious.

At this point, I beg permission to digress. What I have to present here is based on the fact that I, together with others like me, did not experience the days of liberation in war-ruined Germany but in Western Europe, where the fight against Nazism was always *national* at the same time. Further, all of us had a roof over our heads, however sorry our abode may have been at times; and we had something to eat, and, as is well known, eating comes not only before morals but also before any politics. This means, of course, that when I conjure up the memory of 1945 I am distinguishing myself radically from most of the contributors to this volume. They saw only Germany, and that was understandable and legitimate. I didn't see it. I had not the faintest notion of the hardships, of the reconstruction that laid the foundation for the present-day Federal Republic of Germany. For just this reason, perhaps, I am able to muster a certain understanding for the fact that the West Germans in the "Bi-Zone" and later in the emerging Federal Republic were less concerned with freedom, equality, and fraternity than with a house, a bit of bacon for dinner, and a cigarette, and that from such an "objectively historical" situation a mentality arose for which the concept of economics became central.

Now and then on the plane or the Trans-Europe Express I see the sons and grandchildren of the people who were clearing away the rubble in those days. They talk about the business deal they want to "get in on," rummage in their attaché cases, are corpulent and well groomed, while the likes of us are lean and shabby. I find them intensely repugnant. But, for heaven's sake, I am not passing judgment on them. Their teacher was hollow-cheeked want; it taught them to grab and to grin broadly at the unworldly ideologues. They drive big cars, live for the day and leave eternity to God (in whom they certainly believe, without exerting themselves spiritually in the process). They are nouveau riche and nothing frightens them more than poverty, about which their fathers may have told them. Are they of a "restorative" mind? Perhaps. But most likely only in a peripheral way. They pay honor to the old fat but detect clearly that it tastes somewhat rancid. The new fat is aromatic and stirs the appetite. No wonder they prefer it. And, moreover, they tell themselves—provided they have read Goethe—that they are only preserving the inheritance from their fathers in order to possess it. They imagine themselves quite progressive. For progress is for them quantifiable *expansion*, the production that is now being questioned in turn by their own sons, sometimes vehemently.

My digression is at an end. Again I am among my own kind in the epoch of our great illusions, the immediate postwar period. It is interpretable in manifold ways, and the argumentatively strongest interpretations are the Marxist on the one hand, and the purely power-political on the other. The resistance, so it seems to me, was borne by the *élan vital* of a *leftist* view of politics, even when it was nationally tinged. I have in mind not only French Gaullism but also—and this may stir violent objections—the conservative German resistance against Hitler, which reached its climax on July 20, 1944. The officers who roused themselves to topple the Third Reich—no doubt, too halfheartedly and too late—were naturally men of the Right, that is as clear as day. They not only wanted to free Germany from National Socialism (which they had stoutly served!), but at the same time, or above all, they wanted to guard it against Bolshevism. In the global-political sense, their success would certainly not have produced desirable results. If one applies the customary categories—which seem to me, when I ponder them, ever more in need of revision—they were not only conservative but ultrareactionary. Today, more than three decades later and now in full knowledge of the concrete situation, without any illusions, I still persist in believing that their deepest motives, which they certainly would not have wanted to declare and were also hardly aware of, fit the world view of the Left; but only on condition that we are prepared to revise the concept and by the term 'Left' no longer mean an attitude toward the problem of economic hegemony but essentially a radical humanism.

It is yet another matter that the class struggle, which should be understood in a strictly Marxist sense, was still going on at the same time, and if the brave men of the twentieth of July had triumphed, they would have fought it *against* the Left. Here there are more profound and frightening contradictions than Marxist analysis is able to grasp, since they were fought out in the depths of the human soul, and, hélas, there is still nothing that could be called a Marxist psychology. But the German resistance by the men of the twentieth of July, to whom I concede humanistic motives and thus, from my point of view, ultimately leftist motives (that already bear the seeds of a revision of the whole concept of the Left), was only a peripheral phenomenon. At the center was a Résistance that was leftist in the stricter and very strictest sense, that is to say, inspired most decisively and in an unforgettably selfless way by communists. All of us, "le peuple de la nuit," of whom de Gaulle had once spoken in a magnificent speech, thought that it was along with *them* that we would now make a clean sweep of the oppressors. We imagined that the old power structures would collapse by themselves; we would hardly need to nudge what was already toppling anyhow.

Not until 1948 did the Cold War awaken us from our extravagant dreams of liberation. If today one looks back in anger and sorrow, one recognizes how at that time traditional power politics and class politics overlapped to the point of congruence, then separated, only to join again, and why for that reason both interpretations of which I spoke earlier, the Marxist and the realpolitical, are valid. Two superpowers, the only ones to survive as such, the USSR and the USA, confronted one another. In their shadow the classes cowered, ready not for the "last battle" but certainly for a protracted guerrilla war. In the leftist camp, that was bound to produce grave errors, to which I as well as all too many of my friends succumbed. In February 1948 Czechoslovakia, which already in the period between the wars had proven itself to be both a modestly liberal *and* a socialist republic, turned into the People's Democracy that already bore the seeds of the catastrophic events of August 1968. The Right howled. We leftists were silent. The Soviet Union and its vassal Communist parties in East and West appeared to us as the guarantors of the future. After the first all-embracing euphoria of liberation had faded, the USA was in our eyes merely the protector of restoration. It actually was supporting reactionary regimes everywhere. It wanted to rearm Germany. It soon reached the point where Nazi war criminals were treated with kid gloves; the ones who had survived were really the true victors in the Cold War. "The Kaiser went, the generals stayed," Plivier had once written. Hitler was dead, his retainers were alive and set out on a short march through the German institutions, where they settled in forthwith. And if they didn't exactly attain high dignity of office like that unspeakable

Globke, they did enrich the budding German "economic miracle" through the same efficiency with which they had once helped the Führer to carry out his murder plans.

We, the resurrected, stared into the world in foolish disbelief. Many of us were threatened by new persecutions (even if they were by no means comparable to the earlier ones!). To be a victim of the Nazi regime became shameful at a time when McCarthy was setting the tone in the USA and the term "premature antifascism" was coined there. John Foster Dulles was the secretary of state of every European country. The communists had been maneuvered out of the governments of the Western European states. The resistance movement became folklore. Thus one learned to hate. Only all too well, and with shame, do I recall the days when I despised everything American like the plague and on the other hand accepted even the trials against Slansky and Rajk—skeptically, to be sure, but without decided protest. Perhaps they really were traitors, I thought, and added even more pitifully: You can't make an omelet without breaking eggs.

Kravchenko was one of the first to tell how matters really stood in that country about which our communist friends proclaimed in song that "there is no other land on earth / Where human hearts beat so freely." He reported, and we took him to be a paid liar. Arthur Koestler analyzed, and we told ourselves that he was a mercenary of monopoly capitalism. Ignazio Silone appeared on the scene and spoke of his disappointments; we considered him to be a grumbler. And when I say "we," I don't mean the party-member communists, in whose ranks I never marched, but rather the leftists in general and the (not always intelligent) leftist "intellectuals," among whom I proudly counted myself. In truth, we were blind in the left eye. But that I understood only much later, and not fully until Czechoslovakia was raped a second time.

Nonetheless, we can claim extenuating circumstances. The restoration of the old forms of power in Western Europe and especially in the Federal Republic of Germany, where the Nazis were profiting from it, had to discourage us, had to cause us to lose our sense of proportion. The global politics of the United States—"normal" power politics, which Kissinger professed in theory only much later and without great fuss—were having calamitous results in the countries of America's sphere of influence. We understood but poorly that disaster was also descending on the people of the other side. We were so far away. We saw only the sorry figures of the Fourth Republic in France, who traveled to Washington to receive their orders; we saw only Adenauer and Erhard, only a Herr Zehrer, who was romping about briskly upstage, only the Nazi generals who were inspecting American troops, only the Europe of the trusts that had been preconceived by Jean Monnet, only the manifestations of a rabid and unthinking anti-communism. What we failed to see was not only the conditions in the people's democracies, which we regarded at most as the "childhood diseases" of growing socialism, but also the simple fact that people in Western Europe, and especially the Germans, were content with the development for which the Marshall Plan had paved the way. I believe that this was our most consequential error, and for just this error I can find no excuses that would exculpate me.

Despite all the evidence, we convinced ourselves that the nation was unhappy about the restorative trend, which not only integrated and partly even rehabilitated the old Nazis and reactionaries of every variety, but was about to create concrete, consumable prosperity. After all, we had the magic word "alienation" at hand. People were eating themselves full, had rebuilt their houses, were living decently and clothing themselves well. But that did not matter. They were alienated, evidently so much so that they didn't notice how unhappy they were in feeling happy; happy or, at least, halfway content. The wretched of the earth moved into pleasant one-family houses and bought subcompact cars. We scornfully shrugged our shoulders. On the other hand, we waxed enthusiastic about youth festivals in Eastern Bloc countries, over photos from China, where—if one was to believe the pretty, laughing faces—harvesting was pure joy, and over reports about the latest production increase in the Soviet Union.

Were we stupid? By no means! After all, we had read Adorno, Sartre, and Bloch; we dissected concepts with the utmost precision; we "demystified" capitalist society, discerningly penetrated the mechanisms of manipulation; we were talking about "consumer compulsion" and at the same time we ourselves were participating, more or less happily, depending on our skill or elbow power, in the social game of consuming. We acted as though it were not simply up to us not to buy cars but to use a bicycle, not to go along with fashion but to dress like Chinese farm workers. Actually, some of us did that, but it was nothing but a cheap gesture: after all, every one of us had at least a blazer in his closet.

What had stricken us was not stupidity but rather a totally unforgivable intellectual arrogance and an even more unforgivable blindness to the longings, hopes, and fears of our fellow human beings. While the word "concrete" was a key word in our vocabulary, we grew more abstract with each passing day. Alongside us, uninfluenced by our debates and essayistic excesses, history was running its course and with it, naturally, not only the power-political conflict of the superpowers but the class struggle too. The latter, however, was being fought by entrepreneurs and unions, slowly, tenaciously, without dramatic culminations or revolutionary impulses on the one side, or oppression on the other. Therefore, we projected our unrealized revolutionary utopia, which was not shared at all by the people around us, onto the Third World. I remember reading Sartre's preface to Fanon's book *The Wretched of the Earth* with earnest approval. He said that if a colonial kills a colonizer, then two would die, the "oppressor and the oppressed." I believed the *maître* implicitly. The new, socialist man will arise out of revolutionary violence, out of blood and death. Decades later I happened to be in Rome when they found the body of Aldo Moro in a parked car. I witnessed how an entire people condemned the murder in deepest mourning and outrage. In the meantime, I had learned a few other things. For example, the undeniable fact that after the national and allegedly socialist—or why not simply say: national-socialist—revolutions in the developing countries, the new man and the new fraternal society had not been born at all. Dictatorships arose, theocratic fanatic movements emerged, the liberated peoples were afflicted by indescribable misery that was much worse than colonialist oppression (and here I am thinking of Cambodia, but also of Uganda).

The Left was on the spot to protest, fortunately, when it was a matter of battling avowed rightist dictatorships: Chile, Argentina naturally, Iran, and so many others. It remained silent whenever exhaustive and dependable reports spoke not only of the horrors in Cambodia, but also of the oppressive regime in Vietnam, for which they had screamed until their throats were sore. Hadn't those been the good old days when one could still rhythmically yell "hohoho-chi-minh!" Uncle Ho is dead. From the country that claimed to carry on his legacy the people are fleeing without cease on overloaded junks, knowing that their chances of survival are slight and that they will find no refuge. The Left is silent. (Probably, that too is only one of those notorious "childhood diseases of socialism.") It is at hand whenever prisoners suspected of terrorism are mistreated, and I expressly congratulate the Left for such readiness to protest; and I join its protest against the behavior of guardians of public order who take themselves all too seriously. I do it today as I did yesterday and before then too, when I was always ready to endorse the motto: "Wherever there are those who are stronger, always take the side of the weaker." But I don't put up with the one-eyed view of things anymore; precisely because my own left eye was opened very late. I believe that it is necessary to say this. And we must also not succumb to the fear of receiving approval from the wrong quarter. Our anger and sorrow are directed against reactionism, that is clear. But we can no longer overlook those who hand arguments to the fascist and Nazi obscurants, arguments to use as they please. It is high time that we work out a new concept of the Left, and at the proper moment I intend to contribute my small share to the effort.

For I really am concerned with the Left and its further existence. Now as ever, my aversion is directed at the Right, which has shamelessly profited from our preoccupation with abstractions and our one-sidedness. Or does anyone believe that a "Filbinger case" would have been quite so possible if the *people*, neglected by us, had been on our side?[1] I mean the real people, and not some conceptual bugbear. Does anyone think that the Nazis in Germany and the collaborationists in France, Belgium, and Holland could have regained a strong position if we, for our part, had not been compromised on the one hand by a "socialism" to which we understandably but rather unwisely remained loyal, and on the other hand by our unworldly theorizing? The enemy triumphed on all fronts, but not only because it practiced its intrigues in the lee of the United States, not only because soft social democrats were prepared to cooperate with the CIA, also not only because international monopoly capitalism had already assembled right after the war and seized the offensive with concentrated power. If we are where we are today, faced with difficulties, although still not directly threatened, we must ascribe a great part of the blame to ourselves. We were not lacking in "theoretical rigor," but we certainly lacked that lucidity that is not degraded if it is called common sense (a quality that is very unjustly and arrogantly decried as being "banal").

It is this modest but by no means useless mental tool that I am going to employ in jotting down the following few thoughts about the intellectual and political situation in the Federal Republic—which naturally interests our readers most. I realize, of course, that because I live abroad and visit Germany only briefly from time to time, I am an outsider, certainly less informed about the details than any random German newspaper reader. But I don't believe that this peculiar situation disqualifies me from judging German conditions. On the contrary, this very distance enables me to view them from proper perspectives. Otherwise, I would certainly not have decided to write this article.

The Germans, and especially my friends of the Left, don't see the forest for the trees, so to speak. With the help of the international press, which I read faithfully, I recognize from the distance not only the forest but the contours of the hills and mountains too. Thus, I may ask myself what has happened in Germany since the war ended and what is happening there today, trusting that I will find a few reliable answers. I have already alluded to a few things above. At the start, the Germans were not concerned with ideologies, ideals, or utopias but rather with bare survival from one day to the next. Having stated this, I must pause and speak of a commonplace to which I myself fell victim. According to this commonplace, the country suffered from the fact that the middle-class revolution had never been fought through to its end, that twice, in 1918 and 1945, Germany did not attain democracy on its own, but had democracy imposed on it. The notion of the unsuccessful middle-class revolution may be correct; here too, however, the professional historians toss their weighty judgments onto the scale and tell us that a certain element of the revolt by the third estate (for example, religious tolerance) was brought along by the conquering emperor Napoleon in his train and that for this reason alone middle-class freedoms and concurrent national suppression became an insoluble historical contradiction for the Germans.

In 1918 the situation was different. *Wenn wir 1918 . . .* was the title of a book that was much read during the time between the wars. Yes, if in 1918 we had only . . . But at that time, too, the situation was such that revolution would have meant something akin to "foreign rule." Just think of Thomas Mann's deep bitterness right after the war ended! The middle-class revolutionaries were looking toward the West—that was dictating the all too well-known "peace of dishonor"; the emerging proletarian revolutionaries were looking toward the Soviet Union, about which even people like Rosa Luxemburg were very soon having sad thoughts. But no matter, a German revolution would have been thinkable in 1918 and might have given the country a new and better face. Germany was undamaged. The army was "undefeated in the field"; one heard that often enough and joked about it, without asking oneself whether this claim did not contain a tiny kernel of truth. The factories were in working order. Workers' and soldiers' councils could have been constituted and taken over the administration as well as the economy. None of that was unfeasible. What argued against feasibility was not historical logic but facticity. The cadre, impregnated by the stab-in-the-back legend, was not merely antirevolutionary but clearly antirepublican. The dominant powers in the economy and industry were in full possession of their privileges and had no thought of giving them up, especially since they were sure of the approval of the victors in this regard. Still, the question "if in 1918 we had only . . ." was legitimate.

But the constellation in 1945 was totally different. The entire country was occupied. It presented the indelible impression of a tragic landscape of ruins. To be sure, the Western allies were not viewed as political liberators; for the people had accepted the rather cleverly managed Nazi unfreedom with relative indifference. But the victors were helping the hungry. And the fear of the Russians was not only a relic of Goebbels' propaganda but, in considerable measure, also the fruit of a terrible object lesson. A few years after the collapse of the Reich, when the GDR emerged from the "Zone," many a liberal-minded citizen who was happy to be rid of the Nazis could, in regard to East Germany, really echo the words of Kästner: "You can't build a country with these people." In 1945 the German revolution was simply not on the agenda; not only because the occupying powers would have smothered it in any case, but also because the *people* in its overwhelming majority wanted no part of it. One forgets today, because it was so long ago, that Berlin was more than just the "display case of the capitalist masters"; it was very clearly the obvious example for a reality that the masses were better aware of than the leftist intellectuals who were scattered about the country and who were, and have remained, homeless to this day. During the blockade food was brought into the western sector of the city; in the eastern sector people were being forced to attend Marxist training courses.

But do such unalterable facts justify the powers of conservatism and do they expose the women and men of the Left, some of whom had come out of Hitler's concentration camps, as childish dreamers? Naturally not. I am certain that the lack of an authentic Left was responsible for the German calamity: the unorganized of the Left were incapable of aligning with one another and already at that time replacing the SPD with a new socialist party. But this party would absolutely have had to be a party without *illusions*. It would have thrived no better in the intellectual climate of the Frankfurt School than in that of the realism in which the SPD thrived instead. God knows, the SPD still prides itself on having no *ideology* and muddles through from day to day and election to election and, like the old Weimar social democrats, is deathly afraid that its foes might make it out to be a "rootless bunch." Would it have been possible? Nothing is less rewarding than historical retrospection with "if's" and "but's." Inevitably, however, one starts speculating and asks oneself questions that in principle can't be answered. Along the lines of what I have suggested above, one can say that it would have been impossible to create an authentic socialist party. For one, the Western allies would have nipped it in the bud, and, second, the people of West Germany—intent only on sheer survival, maimed by the Russian trauma, and still under the spell of Goebbels' propaganda—would have wanted no part of anything that was even remotely reminiscent of Marxism (which was evil through and through). However, still another development—not probable, but also not impossible—could be imagined: Suppose the "Bi-Zone" and later Federal Republic had tried to make good the middle-class revolution that was never carried out—without terror, guillotine, and corpse carts, but in a single unbloody revolutionary thrust that would overrun the traditional ruling structure. Thanks to its nonviolence, the occupying powers could hardly have prevented it. Such a move actually was included as a possibility in the party platforms, even in that of the CDU. "Demands arising from natural rights" for a new distribution of the great bread loaf of the future would have mobilized the people—not a mythical people, but a very concrete one. Simultaneously, *la patrie, la nation* would have constituted itself in West Germany after the French model. A socialism would have grown out of the ruins, and it would have borne no resemblance to all the disappointing socialist models that we know.

But this is an intellectual game. It was restoration that became reality. It created a country in which one could, and can, live and that was first attacked as "fascistoid" only by those who were its most spoiled, most privileged children: by the young student generation, which was less "alienated" than it cared to admit. To the extent that they were honest with themselves, these young people experienced the "spend-and-buy compulsion" they kept talking about as blissfully as a masochist feels the blows from his self-chosen master. This generation was led by a number of oh so distinguished, refined, esthetically sensitive university professors, who lived, traveled, and did their thinking in luxury. The revolution, or its myth, became a consumer good itself. But the few who felt shame over this miserable state of affairs marched on to what they believed was the real "action." At first, there were only fires in department stores. Soon blood was flowing. When the Germans get serious, things become horrid all over the place.

It was the ruling powers who rubbed their hands, and in Germany that meant those paleo-Nazis who, of course, were already preparing to nurture Neo-Nazis. Nothing could have suited them better than the consumer-revolutionaries who were playing their games in the shade of the restoration on the one hand, and the terror-revolutionaries who had fled directly from their dazed idealism into the realm of the pathological on the other. Cleverly, they not only organized popular rage in the best Goebbels manner but also so intimidated the SPD that the name of the admirable Willy Brandt is now bound up in a really tragic way with one of the government's most stupid and also most ineffective acts—an act, moreover, that damaged the reputation of the Federal Republic abroad to an extent that cannot quite be imagined by German politicians who, drunk with a new feeling of power, tend toward all sorts of excesses. I am speaking, of course, of the *Radicals Decree*, which has been discussed through and through ad nauseam. My readers surely know better than I, who am an outsider in regard to Germany (and also wish to remain one), that this decision is not directed against certain respected lawyers, officials, or aging corporation men with brown or red blemishes on their greedy hands, not against juveniles who find brown or black shirts more becoming than a jeans outfit, not against politicians who are convinced that Herr Rudel's honor as a German soldier not only cannot be impugned but should be presented as a model to the recruits of the *Bundeswehr*. No, the decision directs its entire constitutional rigor against a young teacher who distributed Maoist leaflets ten years ago, against a lawyer who in passing once signed a subversive manifesto, also against a writer who dared to speculate about violence.[2]

Rejuvenating anger stirs at all this. Well, well, they are dragging out the Majdanek trial, quietly hoping that the few surviving witnesses will die off or grow so sclerotic that every miserable scoundrel will have an easy time of ridiculing their testimony; but in the dossiers of tenured high-school teachers who for years have had no other interests but their work and their family, they search for black marks (which they would like to turn into yellow badges). But the anger becomes resigned sorrow when one asks oneself where the old, experienced Left was during the course of events that brought us to where we unfortunately are now, when we are more helpless than ever before. Were we—and I very personally include myself—"on the alert"? Or were we battling as aging Don Quixotes against windmills, while at the same time the enemy battalions were grouping methodically and in line with sanctified tradition? If I look back, it seems to me as though all of us failed pitifully, and not only in Germany. Not few of us had no other concern than the obsessive desire *not to lose touch with the young*. But youth is no more sacred than old age is venerable. Because of its experience and knowledge (which are never the result of personal merit but simply accumulated with time), the older generation, without any claim to wisdom, has the social obligation to teach.

In vain, I ask myself the exacting question of whether we did carry out the work of teaching we were charged with. All of us were in a confused state of mind, caught between resentments, a false feeling of triumph, and unrestrained hopes. We lacked buoyancy. We demanded that the unprotected, unknowing young people agree with everything we say. At the same time, we were eager to concur with everything they were saying, and disregarded the fact that they were still not able to express themselves. Some of the exiles from the Third Reich returned from America. There they had lived in ghettos of emigrés and intellectuals. They did not know that vast land at all, but they presented it as though it were the homeland of both the Babbitts and the bloodthirsty gentlemen from the military-industrial complex. Restorative West Germany, which in no time became a mini-copy of the USA and a kind of trans-Atlantic model farm, was seen through the glasses of the America-weary, who had just experienced McCarthyism. Since they were alien to the giant land, they could not foresee that the Americans would get rid not only of the disastrous senator but, much later, of the considerably more dangerous Nixon, or how they were energetically beginning to solve the race problem. Their false image of America produced in our minds a distorted image of the Federal Republic. Thus, we convinced ourselves and those whom we were supposed to teach that along with all of its NATO partners the Federal Republic was a hell, "as uninhabitable as the moon." Locked within our Neo-Marxist abstract conceptual world, we saw fascistoid manifestations because there were banks and industrial complexes; and in view of such horror we forgot about ordinary fascism, Nazism, to be more exact (for the equation fascism = Nazism is false!). And in a truly unpardonable way we neglected at least partially to enlighten the youth about it. Instead of analyzing historical reality, we erected conceptual houses of cards. With very few exceptions, such as Victor Klemperer, who reflected on the "LTI," the still-unconfronted language of Nazism, we didn't talk about everyday life under the Nazis.[3] Instead, we shrilly screamed "Danger! Fascism!" when an ill-bred minister of economics called the leftist intellectuals "pinschers." The young people screamed along with us. It is not their fault that they lost sight of all proportions. Instead of calmly developing our pedagogical and political strategies, we were shooting at mosquitos with cannons. The masses watched our battle of words with complete indifference. They had what they needed—and some to spare. A Bavarian concentration-camp comrade, a communist, whose superiors had urged him to write articles on the misery of the workers in the Federal Republic, told me resignedly in the early sixties: "I write and write. But the folks say: What the hell do those stupid bastards want, the idiots!" Today I know that the "stupid bastards" were not only the CP functionaries but we too. Someone just moving into his new one-family house was not alienated, but returning home from the alien territory of the rubble. Someone in France who was awakening from the dullness of declining village life and saw arising around Grenoble the industrial complexes that were creating work (and, in addition, four-week vacations, and apartments suitable for human beings) didn't feel he was being "manipulated" by an anonymous machine. He saw new horizons opening. That is why, in May 1968, it was inevitable that the approximately nine million striking workers entered very quickly into serious salary negotiations with the Pompidou government and impatiently dismissed the cascades of words at the Sorbonne and in the Théâtre de l'Odéon with a wave of the hand. We, the older generation, were miserable teachers. Our anger must be directed not only against the enemy of the working class—who was, is, and will remain that, and to this extent we may all safely be Marxists—but above all against ourselves.

The truth is that we failed. That is why we are defenseless today when threats arise such as the Radicals Decree, which I cite merely as an example. What matters now is to make a clean sweep of things, not only among the "oppressed," as the "Internationale" goes, but also in our own triste little circle. We must redefine the concept of the Left for ourselves and then act pragmatically in accordance with it, and pragmatism, of course, does not exclude the grand utopia but rather fills it with real content. Only under these conditions will we be fortified, not for "the final battle," which is still an uncertain matter, but merely for the number of more or less fierce skirmishes that await us and that we must fight to the end, without larmoyance, without persecution obsessions, and without apocalyptic hallucinations. For Hitler is not standing *ante portas*, no matter what sort of nonsense about Germany the French press, which I follow only too closely, is spreading. History does not repeat itself, and even "fascism" (which, by the way, is by far not Nazism) is no immediate threat, not even if *par malheur* that arch-Bavarian, whose name I don't have to mention, were to become the German chancellor.

If I see things correctly, what threatens the Germans is not a tyranny as in Argentina, not to speak of Chile or Nicaragua. Those who have such notions and consequently undertake acts of counterviolence are only playing into the hands of the truly dangerous elements. I mean good old German authoritarianism, which in the days of Kaiser Wilhelm got along without torture and without any signs of physical brutality, so that the Thomas Mann of the *Reflections of a Nonpolitical Man* felt he could profess loyalty to it. Slowly, step by step, they will seek to limit civil liberties. We won't be able to fight that with concepts that say nothing to the people, also not with doom-laden catchwords like the "great refusal." What is incumbent on us is, first of all, the courage of one's convictions, which I miss just as much today as in the years when by speaking frankly one wasn't risking a lucrative career, say, but rather one's neck. In those days, the SA beat us up; today some stupid busybody is sniffing around in our dossier. We must not accept the snooping. On the contrary, we must fight it with all of the means that "formal" democracy places at our disposal. In so doing, we must shun no risk, but we also do not have to imagine immediately that each of us is his own Ossietzky. Our untiring vigilance, our readiness to struggle must not mislead us into shouting "fire" when there are still no flames. The tough, watchful, lucid conduct that common sense dictates has nothing heroic about it. We will have to get along without heroism and plans for personal salvation. That may be regrettable for a few of us, whom they will perhaps try to bar from the media, but there is nothing at all tragic about it. Then we old leftists, who were witnesses, will regain the credibility that we lost and will again have the chance to succeed that, in gloomy moments, we thought was already forfeited.

I believe that what lies before us is not the great drama with the historical culmination point of a bloody last fight. We must reconcile ourselves to fighting limited battles, consisting above all in the patient work of enlightenment. They will become plausible to the populace—they, and not the shrill cries of warning that some of us emit, and surely not the unholy and pathetic conceptual speculations to which nobody listens and that we can always cultivate as a kind of political pastime whenever we hanker for it. Luckily, the Hitler whom we experienced, *we and only we*, and not the young assistants in contemporary history seminars, is simply not present. The old Nazis are dying out with us. Good! Their grandchildren, who are discovering the anti-charm of uniforms and emblems, do not seem to me to be dangerous—not *yet*, even if I don't at all share Martin Walser's opinion that they are nothing but a stupid Mardi Gras bunch. Our dreams from 1945 are dying with us. How sad! But that is the will of historical reality, for which they are only rubbish. But one must not complain. No brown battalions are violently clearing the streets so that they can go stamping through them. New masters with new claims are here. In their overwhelming majority they certainly resemble Monsieur Giscard more than Röhm. We must oppose them with different arguments, indeed, with an entirely new view of the world than the one with which we opposed our adversaries of the years from 1930 to 1933. But who are "we"? We are only the ones who are bowing out, who with the help of statistics can more or less figure out how long our voices will still resound. What matters is those who will come after us. We cannot transmit our experiences to them. But thanks to these very experiences and provided that we have rationally assimilated them, we can give them some advice. We can do it if we bridle our anger (which does not mean that we stifle it!). It may and it will flare up, but this should happen only within the boundaries of our personal experience and memories. At the moment when we publicly address the younger generations our anger must already be transformed into radical reason. If it is unable to undergo this process, it will vanish like smoke, and nothing will remain but a stale smell from bygone days.

Nietzsche the Contemporary

On His Essay "Schopenhauer as Educator"

"SCHOPENHAUER AS EDUCATOR," one of the four parts of *Thoughts Out of Season*, appeared in 1874. At that time Bismarck's Reich was three years old. The works of Karl Marx were already complete, and Sigmund Freud was about to finish the gymnasium. In Germany the first unions were already founded, the years of rapid economic expansion had passed their peak, and many enterprises had been ruined by the stock market crash of 1873. In Vienna Johann Strauss's operetta *Die Fledermaus* had just been performed for the first time. The Third Republic had been established in France, and Great Britain's industrial and imperial power was growing; two years later Queen Victoria became empress.

For the thirty-year-old Friedrich Nietzsche, the pastor's son from Röcken and young university teacher in Basel, 1874 was an unhappy year. But could any year of this life, which aimed to be heroic and yet was one long martyrdom, be called happy? Like his teacher Schopenhauer, Nietzsche scorned the idea of happiness. But the former had a good time of it with his poodle, his genius, and his inveterate arrogance, whereas Nietzsche suffered, sometimes lamentingly

"Nietzsche—der Zeitgenosse: Zu seiner Betrachtung "Schopenhauer als Erzieher," *Merkur* XXIX (December 1975): 1141–49.

and in revolt against his fate, but more often in silence. When he began writing *Thoughts Out of Season*, he really did have little objective cause for contentment—even if it had not been for his neurotic or, as I tend to believe, already latently deranged condition. His early work, *The Birth of Tragedy*, this first grand design of his mythical thought, written between the years 1869 and 1871, had been rejected upon its appearance in 1872 as "unscientific" by the guild of classical philologists, particularly by his teacher Ritschl and by Wilamowitz-Moellendorf, who treated him with even greater severity. His physical state was anything but satisfactory; he really was "always sick in some way after 1873," as Jaspers has expressed it. He was especially plagued by those headaches that in *Doctor Faustus*, for whose title figure Nietzsche was the model, Thomas Mann called with touching ambiguity the "head ache."

It was in such circumstances that *Thoughts Out of Season* was written, the four great essays with which Nietzsche emerged as a social and cultural critic. Of the four, "Schopenhauer as Educator" appears to me to be the most important by far. For this essay contains the entire Nietzsche in a nutshell. It contains everything that still excites us today about this unique thinker but also irritates us: his powerful, suggestive eloquence, which, however, constantly runs the risk of becoming mere loquaciousness; his inclination to megalomania; the intensity of his style, which always borders on a sometimes rather dubious lyricism; his polemical force, which all too easily obscures the actual meaning of the statement; the specifically Nietzschean misanthropy, which the psychologist may trace to a lack of love (since Nietzsche's love for others went unrequited); the verbal excess that still today fascinates some thinkers, while others are struck with fear and trembling when they contemplate such intemperateness.

As regards the content of the essay, I would like to begin by stating that the title is alien to the text, that it is misleading. The reader learns very little about Schopenhauer, even less than someone interested in Flaubert learns about him from Sartre's monumental work on the great author of *Madame Bovary*. When Nietzsche wrote the third part of *Thoughts Out of Season* he had already left the philosophy of Schopenhauer far behind him. What he says about the master—and even quantitatively it is very little—is a projection of his own problems and a pretext for a critical polemic against his time and its trends. Nietzsche did not contribute to making an educator of Schopenhauer.

He could not do it; for he himself was uneducable, a problem child of the spirit, a loner. He talks a great deal about Schopenhauer's solitude, but he means his own:

> He was a hermit through and through; he had not one truly like-minded friend to console him—and between one and none there lies an infinity, as there always does between something and nothing. No one who has true friends knows what true loneliness is, even if the world around him were his enemy.—Oh, I see that you do not know what isolation is. Wherever there were powerful societies, governments, religions, public opinions, in short, wherever there was tyranny, it hated the solitary philosopher; for philosophy provides mankind with an asylum that no tyranny can invade: the cavern of the soul, the labyrinth of the heart.

This is not the solitude of Schopenhauer, who responded with wholesome rage when no notice was taken of him but for the rest leisurely developed his rentier's philosophy of life (which attained its most authentic expression in his unpretentious *Wisdom of Life*).[1] No, this is Nietzsche's own solitude: his threatened health, his ever-precarious financial situation, his life without love—above all, without a woman's love, something that for Schopenhauer would have been nothing but a vexatious burden. And as far as Goethe's "labyrinth of the heart" is concerned, it certainly offered poor Nietzsche no asylum; and what he called the "cavern" was in truth more a hell.

If I say that the text under discussion here already contains the entire Nietzsche in a nutshell, I have to explain what I see in it that is so typical or foretelling for this thinker and his subsequent development. And this brings me first of all to the *superman*. In "Schopenhauer as Educator" he still is not called that. But he is already present. Nietzsche says that it must be the goal of mankind to give rise to the "genius." Nothing is more repulsive to him than Bentham's formula of the "greatest happiness of the greatest number." "Oh, Philistine," he cries out angrily, "as though it could make more sense to permit numbers to decide when it is really a matter of worth and meaning!" The tendency toward quantification that social philosophy took over from the natural sciences is for him a scandal. What alone matters to him is that humanity ceaselessly strive to produce individual great men. This demand is raised again and again with irritating urgency. It contains, to be certain, no more and no less than the essence of Nietzsche's criticism of his time and its culture.

Creation of the superman: that in itself already implies the reevaluation of values; for when Nietzsche speaks of the "great man," he means neither the statesman of genius (for example, Bismarck, whose name is not mentioned) nor the researcher of genius (in some special field or other); he does not even mean the artist (in the sense of the Romantic notion of genius). The great man, as an ideal type, is recognized and identified in Schopenhauer. But Schopenhauer is only a mask. Behind the surly face of this man, who is always referred to as the "old one" (since it is absolutely impossible to imagine him as young), we find Nietzsche's own face, the face of the Gallic warrior. The genius is Nietzsche himself. The text reveals the particularities of his entire later work also in that it has a decidedly subjective, even autobiographical character. When Nietzsche speaks of the world he means himself; when he says "culture" he has his own world of thought in mind. Friedrich Nietzsche's entire work is nothing but an attempt at introspection, self-portraiture, self-stylization—to be sure, however, a brilliantly successful attempt. Whoever wishes is free to speak of a "narcissistic neurosis," but the psychological concept would not detract from the vast dimensions of his impressive as well as vexing work.

In a certain, of course strictly limited, sense, Nietzsche actually does prove himself in this work to be a disciple of Schopenhauer: in his total, uncompromising scorn of those whom Schopenhauer called the far-too-many. He has as little use for them, for the man on the street (to employ a modern American expression), as the established order had for him. He regards the "pursuit of happiness," which remains the basis of every democratic, liberal society, as nothing but an insolent presumption. Mankind, a lowly species, has not grasped that its sole task is to promote the rise of the "true man." It deserves the whip of Nietzsche's philosophy, the "hammer" with which this thinker imagines he is philosophizing, whereas in the last analysis he is merely lamenting and accusing.

Nevertheless, in his lamentations and accusations Nietzsche, as expression of Hegel's *Weltgeist*, combines his personal subjectivity with objectively warranted criticism of his epoch. Let us pause for a moment in order once again to remind ourselves what Nietzsche's times were like. In the case of Germany they are marked by an extraordinary self-complacency that rapidly shifts from euphoria to satiety. Despite the bank crash, occasional economic recessions, and awakening consciousness among the working class, the people are in accord with capitalism triumphans. The great war was won. The Reich is splendidly armed. What more could anyone want?

If one is a Nietzsche, one wants much more and also something completely different. Above all, this Reich, which is the pride of the "far-too-many," means nothing at all to him. Binding, an author with Nietzschean pretenses, writes that the first words he can recall his father saying were "Reich und Kaiser." Nietzsche, who could have been Binding's father, said the following about the Reich in "Schopenhauer as Educator":

> There are at the moment naïve people . . . in Germany who . . . say that for a few years now all has been well with the world, and that whoever cherishes heavy, dark doubts about life is disproved by the "facts." Because the truth is that the foundation of the new German Reich is the decisive victory blow against all the "pessimistic" philosophizing. . . . It is a deep disgrace that such disgusting, idolatrous praise of these times can be uttered or repeated by so-called thinking and honorable people.

So much for the Reich. And there is not even mention of the Kaiser. There is mention, however, of triumphant capitalism, even if Nietzsche is obviously not familiar enough with the economic term to employ it. For when he says that the "tremendous migration of peoples over this huge earth, their founding of cities and states, their wars, their confused gatherings and dispersions, their chance amalgamations, their learning from one another, their mutual deceptions and oppressions" are "the continuation of the animal state," then he has his own epoch in mind, the *saeculum obscurum*, as he not unjustifiably describes his century. It is the world of capitalism that has made deception and oppression its law, and the successful capitalistic oppressor and deceiver is merely the repulsive caricature of the "great man," as Nietzsche sees him.

Other passages make his criticism of capitalistic society even clearer. We read that the quantitative principle of education is just as dangerous as "the economic doctrine of laissez-faire [is] for the morality of entire peoples." But Nietzsche is most unequivocal when he speaks of the "selfishness of the profit-seekers" and exposes the capitalistic formula of property plus education as a mystification. In his own words: "Firstly, there is the selfishness of the profit-seekers, something that requires the help of culture and helps culture in return, while at the same time wishing to dictate its goals and limits." The word "manipulation" was still not part of the German vocabulary, but the fact itself could not be overlooked. Nietzsche clearly recognized it. Let us listen further:

> From them [the profit-seekers] comes that favorite tenet and sorite that more or less states: as much knowledge and education as possible; thus, the greatest possible need for it; thus, the greatest possible production; thus, the greatest possible profit and happiness.—So goes the seductive formula. Its proponents would define education as the insight that enables one to be truly modern in one's needs and their satisfaction but that also gives one command of every means and method of making money as easily as possible. The aim would be to create lots of "current" people, in the sense of "currency" as it is applied to money. According to this view, a nation will be all the happier the more such "current" people it has.

Is not this "current" person the same one who nowadays is called "alienated"? And was not all of education—and here it is a matter of education and educational institutions—the same education whose repressive function is the subject of today's debates? Nietzsche is protesting against the false alliance of "intelligence and property," of "wealth and culture." This truly shows him to be a "man out-of-season," a reevaluator of values in opposition to his epoch—which I have described as the period of capitalism triumphans. If one wishes, one can call Nietzsche's "current man" the "average man" (as statistics construe him); one would also be justified in calling him the "one-dimensional" man. In any event, the "current man" is Nietzsche's contemporary, the product and supporter of capitalistic society, who is content if he is granted just that much culture as is required to serve the interests of "general and world trade." Needless to say, the "culture" envisioned by Nietzsche and that already appears dimly on the horizon in "Schopenhauer as Educator" is incompatible with what his contemporaries called culture or civilization. His culture is not the culture of the scholars, who, he says, are shielded from all "artificial and excessive hypotheses." Nor is it the culture that he scornfully describes as one of wealth, refinement, and well-mannered dissemblance. Nietzsche's culture is excess, dissipation, immoderation through and through, a culture of "fire," as he very expressly says with reference to Richard Wagner. Nietzsche's conception of culture, both esthetic and moral-amoral, must be understood as the antithesis of the culture or civilization of his day, as a protest against the image of man with which contemporary capitalism presented him.

But it is high time to avert misunderstandings. Far be it from me

to see a kind of frustrated Marxist in the Nietzsche whom we encounter in "Schopenhauer as Educator." Nothing could be more dem-
agogic and foolish than that. Everyone knows that Nietzsche was as
opposed to the wishful thinking of the socialism of his epoch as he was
to bourgeois democracy; but he rejected the latter much more radically
than the former. For it was not just democracy that provoked his hate
and scorn but the state altogether. That makes him a forerunner of the
modern anarchistic anthropology that is being sent us from France
these days and is associated with the names Michel Foucault and Giles
Deleuze (two thinkers, by the way, who constantly make reference to
him). He writes of the state and its cultural presumption in
"Schopenhauer as Educator":

> There is . . . the *selfishness of the state*, which desires the greatest dissemina-
> tion and popularization of culture, and possesses the most effective tools for
> achieving its ends. If it feels strong enough not only to unleash but also at
> the right time to harness, if its foundation be firm and broad enough to bear
> the entire educational structure, then the spread of education among its
> citizens will benefit the state in its competition with other states. Wherever
> there is now talk of a "civilized state," this state has the task of freeing the
> spiritual wishes of a generation, to the degree that they can serve and
> benefit the existing institutions—but only to this degree.

These are highly modern thoughts! By no means is Nietzsche
speaking here of the state we describe today as "totalitarian," but
rather of the bourgeois-capitalistic society that he knew and that was
formed into a state in Wilhelmine Germany in the same way as it was
in the Western democracies. Already here it becomes apparent how he
would have viewed the totalitarian state. It may be, however, that—as
the party philosopher of the Third Reich, Alfred Bäumler, tried to
prove—he would have welcomed the state of the blond beasts, with
their military triumphs and their eugenic "Lebensborn."[2] I don't believe that he would have, but it is not entirely unimaginable. —Please
pardon the digression. A most repulsive thought forced itself upon me;
I wrote it down, but I absolutely doubt its probability. I see Nietzsche
as the forebear not of Nazi barbarism but rather of a subjectivistic-
anarchistic rebellion against the masses. Wherever we read in
"Schopenhauer as Educator" we discover a vehement polemic against
everything that is concealed behind the concept of a mass society, a
concept that may be unclear but, not without good reason, has become

part of linguistic usage. Again and again we encounter formulations of a kind common to the discourse of our own time, as, for example, when Nietzsche says that the people of his day are "the tormented slaves of the moment, the prevailing views, and the fashions." Today we would say: of relevance, manipulation, and conformism.

Nietzsche becomes our contemporary, too, when he ridicules the intellectual dictatorship of both the natural sciences and history, but at the same time settles accounts with the speculative-constructive metaphysics of German idealism:

> Earlier, especially in Germany, the philosophers were so deep in thought that they were constantly in danger of running into the wall. Now they have about them, as Swift tells us of the Laputans, a whole swarm of flappers to give them an occasional light stroke on the eyes or someplace else. . . . The flappers are the natural sciences and history . . .

The age he lived in but whose beliefs he repudiates and again and again tries desperately to break away from is, let us not forget it, that point in history when the still-budding natural sciences believed they were about to solve everything that they called the "riddle of the universe." Vogt, Moleschott, Ludwig Büchner enjoyed high esteem. Ernst Haeckel was about to appear on the scene with his monistic-scientific world view. The humanities, on the other hand, had taken flight into the past. Nietzsche had ample occasion to witness this phenomenon in the person of Jakob Burckhard in Basel.

The state of philosophy, Nietzsche's foremost concern, was wretched. He looks about and sees, as he writes, only "a ridiculous herd of poor philosophers" who are about to turn philosophy "into a ridiculous matter." He sees one of the chief causes for this lamentable state of philosophy in what we would describe today as the "appropriation" of the philosophers by society:

> As long as we have this state-sanctioned sham thinking, the grand effects of a true philosophy will be thwarted. . . . For this reason I believe it is a cultural necessity to deny philosophy all state and academic recognition and to relieve both state and academy of the impossible task of differentiating between true and false philosophy. Let the philosophers sprout where they can; deny them any prospect of employment or integration into the civic professions; don't tickle them with rewards; indeed: persecute them, be unkind to them.

Naturally, this is the voice of Schopenhauer's admirer, of the man whose teacher did not launch a successful university career, not so much because of some grim decision but because of the disgraceful fact that the students did not enroll in his courses but flocked next door to Hegel instead. It is also the voice of the young professor of philology at the University of Basel, who recognized very clearly that if he wanted to teach philosophy he would hardly have an easier time of it than his master, and for this reason finally chose an independent career as a writer. A psychological explanation of this sort may get at the motives, but it misses the content of Nietzsche's diatribe, which must be understood within the context of intellectual history. If we disregard Nietzsche the person, forever wounded in his honor and therefore irritated, we will immediately perceive his radical, almost anarchistic *rejection:* rejection of the state, of public opinion, of society—whose overwhelming integrating power he recognized. His demand for "free-sprouting" philosophers, who enjoy no official recognition, are treated ill by society, if need be even persecuted, is by no means as absurd as it must have appeared to his contemporaries. He demanded what has been partially realized in our own century: thinkers outside the institutions, men like Sigmund Freud, who never gained an academic professorship, like Oswald Spengler, a private scholar, like Jean-Paul Sartre, who showed interest in the academic enterprise only to the extent that he wanted to contribute to its destruction.

I believe that the essay "Schopenhauer as Educator" contains *in nuce* not only the entire later Nietzsche, but that in all of its vexing and vexed content, including its distinct megalomaniacal and autistic features, it points beyond Nietzsche's own time into ours. Above all, it marks the break in the history of ideas that Nietzsche's entire work represents. We clearly discern the discontinuity that this thinker brought about. For Nietzsche was the man who burned all the bridges behind him, as it were. After Nietzsche there can be no return to Christianity, to the idealistic philosophy and humanism of the eighteenth century. He stands not only "beyond good and evil," but beyond all tradition. Schopenhauer was influenced by Kant, Marx by Hegel; but Nietzsche appeared from nowhere, armed with the truly "hammering" mind of a man who was fated to madness. We must accept him for what he was: the prophet of a new day that never dawned, of a joyful wisdom that was not achieved, of a dance that was never danced. His work contains dreadful pronouncements. He says, for example, that it is more important that a philosopher arise on this earth than that a state and a philosophy go on existing. Or he calls out in his highly agitated, unconsidered, even thoughtless way that Brutus offers greater proof for the dignity of philosophy than Plato. In "Schopenhauer as Educator" we also find what is the keystone of his thought: "[Philosophy] should be something fearful; and those chosen to strive for power should know the source of heroism that flows in it."

Fearfulness, hammer, power, heroism: such words came all too easily to this sickly man who longed so much and so vainly for free physis, who would not hurt a fly, and who in the end went insane while embracing a flogged cab horse. He was not only the enemy of the state and society but also the adversary of the image of man inherited from antiquity and elevated during the Enlightenment to the pinnacle of modernity. Almost a century after him structuralism is talking about the "death of man." Every newspaper reader has a seat at the deathbed of mankind. The essay "Schopenhauer as Educator" guides us on the shortest path not only into Nietzsche's world of thought but also into our own present.

The Limits of Perspicacity
On *Ludwig Wittgenstein's* Culture and Values

A proof that God exists should really be something by means of which one can convince oneself of God's existence. But I imagine that the *believers* who provide such proofs wanted to analyze and substantiate their "beliefs" through reasoning, although they themselves would have never arrived at belief as a result of such proofs. Perhaps it would be possible to convince someone of "God's existence" through a kind of upbringing, by forming that person's life in a particular way. Life can educate a person to belief in God. And *experiences* likewise accomplish this. It is not visions or other sensory experiences that show us the "existence of this being," but rather, for example, various kinds of suffering. And they do not show us God as a sensory impression shows us an object, nor do they permit us to surmise his existence. Experiences, thoughts, life can force this concept upon us. Then it resembles somewhat the concept "object".

WHO WROTE THAT? Who can be speaking here of the doctrine of suffering that enables us to experience God? Who is desperately attempting to lend him concrete form through suffering? A modern theologian? Naturally. Well, that is what one would "naturally" expect, but unfortunately it is not so. This voice belongs to none other than Ludwig Wittgenstein, whose *Tractatus Logico-Philosophicus* was

"An den Grenzen des Scharfsinns: Zu den *Vermischten Bemerkungen* Ludwig Wittgensteins," *Neue Rundschau* XC, 1 (1979): 86–95.

once the bible of the neopositivists, a man who wished to convince an entire generation that a language purified by logic is the mirror of the logical construction of the world; a man who knew enough about mathematics to recognize its metaphysical background; a perspicacious theoretician of knowledge who wished to "treat" philosophy the way one treats "an illness" and who exorcized from the debate (as if they were evil spirits) all those pronouncements that he viewed as "sense-less"; a man who advanced the enormous claim that for every true question an answer could be found, and that there is no such thing as a riddle.

Certainly, no one familiar with this philosopher, who despised the philosophy of his day and preferred reading American detective novels to professional journals, this Ludwig Wittgenstein, who was an Austrian, Jew, and Catholic and who had already assumed a different position when his *Tractatus* gained world renown, will be astonished by such a theological excursus. In the *Philosophical Investigations*, his second, less-known major work, Wittgenstein retracted most of the theses of the *Tractatus*, liberated himself entirely from the empiristic element of positivism and, as it were, locked humankind in language, or what he called the "language games."[1] In his latter years, the thinker, architect, and amateur musician, who was born in Vienna in 1889, approached what already in the *Tractatus* he called in sibylline allusion the "mystical." Russell's pronouncement that "logic's hell" (which should not be translated with such thoughtless literality as was unfortunately done in German with "Die Logik ist die Hölle") became a reality in Wittgenstein's person. His perspicacity reached its limits. Beyond them lay the realm of the mystical-religious, but also the realm of madness.

> If in life we are surrounded by death, so too are we surrounded by madness although our reason still be sound. . . . Is it perhaps an unfulfilled longing that drives a person mad? . . . One does not have to regard madness as a sickness. Why not as a sudden—a more or *less* sudden—change of charac-ter? . . . I often fear madness. Do I have any reason to assume that this fear does not originate in an optical illusion, so to speak; do I take something to be a near abyss that is really not one at all? The only *experience* I know of that tells me for certain that it is no illusion is the case of Lenau. In his *Faust* there are thoughts of a kind that I am also familiar with. Lenau has Faust think them, but they are surely his own about himself. What Faust says about his *loneliness* or *solitude* is important.

This is what we find in the posthumous *Culture and Values*,[2] a collection of notes or observations assembled by Wittgenstein's disciple Georg Henrik von Wright with considerable effort but probably not intended for publication by the author. They extend from 1929 to 1951 and are indispensable parerga and parilipomena for experts on Wittgenstein's work, but their readership should by no means be limited to the experts. The book contains notes on music, architecture, Judaism, ethics, and, of course, philosophy, and will also interest people who do not know Wittgenstein's work or know it only from hearsay. It is a bit like with Schopenhauer: one need not necessarily have studied *The World as Will and Representation* in order to gain insight from *The Wisdom of Life*.[3] It is only natural, however, that someone who really knows Wittgenstein will derive more from these random notes, which the editor often deciphered only with difficulty, than the lay Wittgenstein reader or someone reading him for the first time— particularly things that supplement his inner and outer biography. For this reason I will very briefly sketch the biographical information needed for understanding Wittgenstein's posthumous writings.

Who was he? He was the son of one of Austria's richest steel industrialists. He was a Jew according to the racial notions of the Third Reich, a Catholic by religious upbringing and, later, by virtue of his spiritual development. He gave the gigantic fortune that he inherited to his sisters and saw to it that he died as poor as a beggar. The *loneliness* or *solitude* of which he wrote and in which he saw implicitly the work of madness, was not a fate imposed from without but—in the existential sense!—his own free choice. He did not pursue a profession in keeping with his family background and his connections; rather he lived a life of monastic asceticism. For a time he was a grade-school teacher in a small Lower Austrian community, a hermit in Scandinavia, even a gardener in a monastery. When Bertrand Russell discovered him through the *Tractatus* as a great logician and prepared the way for his activity as a university lecturer in England, he accepted reluctantly. Had not Hitler's annexation of Austria in 1938, when he was already living in England, taken him by surprise, he probably would never have become a British citizen. For he did not love the country that helped him to world fame. To the end, he remained an Austrian, infected by the *morbus austriacus*. Should one note that three of his brothers committed suicide? One hesitates; for this observation would place the existential freedom of his decision to live in solitude in question, and explain his fear of madness as a genetically determined fate. But was his fear not *already* madness? And on the other hand, what *is* madness? One may certainly note that another of his brothers was the one-armed pianist Paul Wittgenstein, who could afford to commission a piano concerto for the left hand from Maurice Ravel. Ludwig Wittgenstein himself lived in more intimate association with music than philosophy, and in his notes we find an example of musical notation. Music, too, which he tried to capture in metaphorical speech, belonged to the realm of the "mystical," of which one was not supposed to talk, but of which he spoke nonetheless. For as he writes in the *Tractatus:* "The limits of my language are the limits of my world." And since music was his world, he extended the limits of his language beyond it—impermissibly, in fact. Here are a few examples that show his earnest striving and at the same time his helplessness, his vulnerability:

> Understanding and explaining a musical phrase. The simplest explanation sometimes is a gesture; another might be a dance step, or words that describe a dance. But is not understanding the phrase an experience while we are hearing it? And of what use is the explanation? Are we to think of it as we are listening to the music? Are we supposed to picture the dance, or whatever, while listening? And if we were to do it, why should *that* be called listening to music with understanding?

Here it is still the logician Wittgenstein who is speaking, the logician who no longer trusts language, including language cleansed by logic, and who refers us to direct physical experiences. It is the same Wittgenstein who despaired of all possibility of *explanation*. Elsewhere he dispensed entirely with discursive-analytic speech and merely hinted metaphorically at what he had personally experienced:

> What is missing in Mendelssohn's music? A "courageous melody."
> One could call Wagner's motifs musical prose sentences. And just as there is "rhymed prose," one can join these motifs together in melodic form, but they won't produce *one* melody.

Such pronouncements naturally say nothing about Wagner or Mendelssohn, or Brahms, whom he esteemed highly, or Beethoven, whom he revered. But they say a great deal about Wittgenstein. Above all, we must note his constantly recurring remarks on Mendelssohn. Because Mendelssohn was a *Jew*. Precisely on account of this, Wittgenstein credited him with as little genuine and independent creative power as he did himself, and for the very same reason.

That Wittgenstein grappled with the problem of Jewish identity so intensively and in so personal a way, or better really, let it engulf him, was new to me, and because of that all the more gripping. He was strongly influenced by the now-forgotten philosopher Otto Weininger, a self-hating Jew who, if not a genius, was certainly touched by genius. Weininger could not bear his origins and with supreme logic shot himself as a young man. Wittgenstein, raised as a Catholic, very Austrian in his view of himself, feeling more affinity to Lenau than to Sigmund Freud, to whose ideas he had, so to speak, a respectful aversion, did not go so far as the unhappy author of the once so sensational work *Sex and Character*. He did not kill himself like his brothers, though it is possible that the cancer of which he died merely intervened before he could take his own life. However that may be, it emerges clearly from his notes that he suffered from being Jewish. More than that: it becomes clear that one can properly understand him as a person only when one attempts to place him within the context of Austrian Jewry. How did he see the Jew and thus himself? Not exactly as a parasite, which the very primitive antisemitic propaganda of his time claimed the Jew to be, and also not as evil incarnate, as did the mentally disturbed Weininger. But he did see him as someone who is "different," as a reproductive spirit at best. *Genius* was something that he denied Jews: the Jew Mendelssohn, the Jew Freud, himself. "The only Jewish 'genius' is a saint. The greatest Jewish thinker is only a talent. (I, for example.) I believe that there is truth to the idea that my thinking is really only reproductive."

He saw himself wrongly; he was belittling himself. For, as Sartre put it much later, he had allowed the enemy to determine his self-image. Was not *he* the original thinker? Did *he* not inspire the "Aryan" Bertrand Russell, even though Russell regarded the work of his latter years with the same skepticism as the author of this essay? Was it not *he*, with his *Tractatus*, who had stimulated the thinking of the official head of the Vienna Circle, the "Aryan" Moritz Schlick, who remained more loyal to him than he did to himself? And was it not Schlick from whom all those impulses came that for decades dominated Anglo-Saxon and, above all, American philosophy, with a virtual claim to exclusivity? At this point I will dare to speculate rather boldly and ask myself: Would not Wittgenstein perhaps have stood by the basic thoughts of the *Tractatus* to the end if he had not felt stigmatized by the blemish of being a Jew, which robbed him of his ultimate, that is, his biological self-confidence?

> In a real sense, the Jew can trust in nothing. But this is most difficult for him because he has nothing, as it were. It is much harder willingly to be poor when one *must* be poor than when one could be rich. The reason that the history of the Jews is not treated as extensively within the history of the peoples of Europe as the Jews' intrusion into European affairs would merit, is that they are felt to be a sickness and anomaly within this history and no one likes to speak of a sickness as though it were equal in value to the body's healthy (even painful) processes. . . . From the individual one can . . . expect tolerance, or that he disregard such things; but not from the nation, which owes its existence as a nation to the very fact that it does not disregard such things. That is to say: It is a contradiction to expect someone to retain his former esthetic feeling for his body *and* at the same time to welcome a boil on it.

What does this mean? It surely means that in his quality as a Jew Wittgenstein viewed himself as a boil on the body of the Austrian nation; furthermore, that for this reason he could muster no more than tolerance for himself and that he did not rest secure in a spiritual-esthetic consciousness of existence. Here we have a key to understanding the man and thinker Wittgenstein (and I cannot but wonder at the blissful unawareness of international criticism, which has not examined this phenomenon). It may be *the* key, and I could cite more to substantiate my thesis than is possible here. But we must go on to other, more objective factors, although I insist that Wittgenstein, above all, is one of those spirits who cannot properly be dealt with unless one examines their biography. The most significant quality in which Wittgenstein "differs" is probably his attitude toward science, as we see it in his posthumous notes. To start with, I call to mind one of the basic theses of the *Tractatus*. It begins with a sentence that has been quoted to a surfeit: "The world is everything that is the case." Already with this pronouncement, which is mathematically numbered and further developed in the work with the greatest logical stringency, Wittgenstein rejects every kind of metaphysical speculation, banishes all ontology as nonsense. Whatever "is the case" can be expressed and examined in the manner of the exact sciences. The rest is what he cryptically calls the "mystical," about which one cannot speak.

Striking is his faith in the seemingly unlimited possibilities of the natural sciences, in which Wittgenstein's pupils, the neopositivists, and among them especially Schlick (who was also a physicist) and Otto von Neurath, had believed as though it were the *ultima ratio*. Their and Rudolf Carnap's stimulation gave rise to the world view of "physicalism," with its principle that all meaningful statements on reality had to be reducible to statements on physical reality expressed in mathematical language. For logical reasons, as he said (or because of ontological errancy, as I suspect), already in the posthumously published *Philosophical Investigations* Wittgenstein had greatly distanced himself not only from true physicalistic neopositivism but also from the thinking, based on the writings of Popper, that later became critical rationalism.

Wittgenstein's notes pertinent to this discussion make all the more clear to what degree he exchanged the logically founded scientific world view he had previously advocated for what he once called the "mystical," i.e., something not to be spoken about. Now he talks, or stutters, questioningly about the inexpressible. His rejection of science is amazing; it assumes such proportions as we know only from the case of Heidegger, who uttered the monstrous words: "Science does not think"—as though Einstein, Planck, Heisenberg, and, more recently, Jacques Monod or Ilya Prigogine had arrived at their scientific insights somewhere beyond thinking!

> It is . . . not absurd to believe that the scientific and technical age is the beginning of the end for humanity; that the idea of great progress is a delusion, just as it is a delusion that man will ultimately know truth; that there is nothing good or desirable about scientific knowledge and that mankind, by striving for it, is running into a trap.

Now then, this is no less, but also no more, than that long since familiar pessimism about the future of civilization that has lately returned to fashion. Here, however, unlike the contemporary version, its arguments are not even sociocritical or political. Wittgenstein was personally too introverted to be able to examine critically the fate imposed on all of us by society. It is most conspicuous in this regard that he does not mention the name Karl Marx a single time—he, the Austrian, who solely by virtue of the Austrian intellectual climate between the two World Wars certainly should have been familiar with "Austro-Marxism," which accomplished so tremendously much for the social restructuring and, not least, social planning of his native city, Vienna. But Marx happened to be concerned with history and society, and so he was apparently of no concern to Wittgenstein, i.e., to the individual with his private property (as Stirner would have it). On the other hand, the name Freud turns up repeatedly: "The prose style of (the logician and mathematician) Frege is sometimes *great;* Freud writes excellently and it is a pleasure to read him, but he is never *great* in his writing."

Well, that is, of course, nonsense. Every literary historian and critic of style agrees that, quite apart from the content of his writing, Freud was, after Schopenhauer, the greatest philosophical writer in the German language. But for Wittgenstein he could not be great, since greatness is a dimension that no Jew is permitted to achieve.

A good deal has been said about the phenomenon of Jewish "self-hate." The concept applies perfectly to Karl Kraus, whom Wittgenstein repeatedly mentions with respect in his posthumous notes. It can be applied to Wittgenstein himself only with reservations. Being Jewish distressed him; not least for this reason he constantly doubted himself and his significance. But it would be false to say that he hated himself for that reason, as did a Weininger, or a Kraus, who projected his self-hate outwardly on a grand scale and directed it against the Jewish liberal newspaper *Neue Freie Presse*. Wittgenstein was no hater at all, not a "good" one in the Nietzschean sense; even less was he a bad, perfidious one. He was an unhappy man. And he was unhappy because, above all, he not only did not believe in science, but he also did not believe in philosophy, which he practiced and taught.

"For the philosopher there grows more grass in the valleys of slow wit than on the bare heights of cleverness." What a terribly strange and yet most revealing sentence! How is one to interpret it? It seems to me that Wittgenstein scorned "cleverness" (i.e., analytic, discursive thinking) in his late years because he had tried, if you will, all the possibilities of ratio, or he had strayed from it, as can be argued just as well. What he was searching for, after he had explored the "bare heights of cleverness," was something on the order of the "good and sound" life that does not brood about itself. He believed it could be found in the valleys of a "slow wit" that he should rather have designated as "simplemindedness." But he should have known better after he had already searched in vain for the healthy simplicity of the heart in his young days as a village schoolteacher. His posthumous writing teaches us that this philosopher of the most extremely consistent logical exactitude was the precise opposite of what his friend Bertrand

Russell, who was certainly ironic but still dwelt deeply within himself, embodied in his own person. Even in his radicalism Bertrand Russell was at bottom a man of moderation, of restraint, and above all: he was rooted externally and internally. Wittgenstein was a restless wanderer—of the spirit and in the world. Perhaps no other pronouncement expresses his state of being better than the following, which in regard to its content and diction could be by Franz Kafka: "It seems as if I had gotten lost and asked someone the way home. He says that he will guide me and walks with me along a lovely, smooth path. Suddenly it comes to an end. And now my friend says: 'All you have to do now is to find your way home from here.'"

I already know, no one has to tell me: This can be interpreted in strictly philosophical terms. Thus, the path would be the thought process, which proceeds in a series of purely logical operations, and the sudden isolation, symbolized by the statement of the friend, would be the point at which logical-tautological speech closes the circle within itself and we are given the task of going home as an approximation to the ultimate, the transcendental things, which lie beyond language and the possibility of precise thought. There may be something to this; but as far as I am concerned, I rather tend to see an autobiographical-existential parable in this note from the year 1945. The empirical Ludwig Wittgenstein no longer has a "home"—in contrast to Lord Russell, who was not faced with the problem of home because he possessed one, no matter if he loved it or not. Wittgenstein's homeland, Austria, no longer existed. Had it ever existed? (Try asking Robert Musil: For him his "Kakanien" was only an ironic figure of thought; he, too, did not know where he belonged.) But beyond the empirical Wittgenstein, who was homeless, there was the "transcendental" Wittgenstein, as it were, who for his part, of course, gave expression to his metaphysical troubles (which cannot be comprehended in strictly philosophical terms). To describe this Wittgenstein one must take recourse, as he himself did, to metaphorical speech. I mean the spiritual wanderer Wittgenstein, who, like the surveyor in Kafka's *Castle*, never reaches his goal, perhaps because it actually does not even exist. Both of them, the empirical and the transcendental Wittgenstein, remained on a path—is it perhaps Heidegger's "wrong track"?—that runs into a dead end; and from such a non-path there is no way to get "home."

Ludwig Wittgenstein did not return from his journey: neither to the newly arisen Austria that today looks so pretty and flirtatious but in its depths and abysses is the way Thomas Bernhard described it in his novel *Die Korrektur* (in which he etched the features of the man Wittgenstein into the figure of the mathematician Roithammer); nor did he find a path back to the logic that mirrors the structure of the world and that the *Tractatus* proposed as the outermost reference point of all thought and investigation. Basically, he had never truly and wholeheartedly believed in this logic and its sovereignty as did his friend Lord Bertrand Russell—with whose thinking he no longer agreed. If he had, he would never have recorded words like the following—already in 1933!—with which our deliberations will conclude, leaving a great many question marks behind the final sentences:

> If someone believes he has found the solution to the problem of life and wished to tell himself that now all is simple, he can convince himself that it isn't so merely by recalling that there was a time when this solution hadn't been found; but also at that time, too, he had to be able to live, and looking back on it the discovered solution appears to be accidental. . . . If there were a "solution" to the problems of logic (philosophy), we would have to remind ourselves that at an earlier time they weren't solved (and at that time, too, one had to be able to live and think).

Simone Weil

Beyond the Legend

IN GOD ALL contradictions are resolved, claim the theologians along with Nicholas of Cusa. But on this miserable earth they are by no means resolved. They tear apart the individual and society. Simone Weil is the tragic example for the impotence of the *deus absconditus* in the face of the world's contradictions. Her thirst for the absolute literally withered her. Everything relative—origins, social station, education—was her downfall. She wanted to live wholly for others; her hardly surpassable egocentrism enveloped her as though she had been poured into amber. She aspired toward the eternal but the times formed her and finally turned her into a sacrificial animal. Her spirit dwelt aloft somewhere in the thinnest air of purity; her physical appearance was neglected and gave some people the impression that she was dirty. She hated Judaism, and externally as well as in her character make-up, she was extravagantly Jewish. She wanted to be a worker, but she was incapable of satisfactorily performing even the most rudimentary manual task. She felt that she was destined to be a hero, but when she went to Spain in order to take part in the Civil War, she clumsily scorched herself with boiling oil and had to be returned home straightaway by her caring parents. She succeeded

"Simone Weil—Jenseits der Legende," *Merkur* XXXIII (January 1979): 80–86.

only in dying. And when this passionate Christian mystic was buried in Ashford, England, she was not baptized and not even a priest was there to bless her remains. Because of an air-raid alarm, the man of God had missed his train.

To make her out is no easy matter, for legends have obscured her being and work. Hagiography took the place of critical biography. Charles de Gaulle, who was no mean judge of people, said tersely that she was *folle*, crazy. But Camus, oppressed by the transcendent and transcendental basic human condition, spent an hour of meditation in her Paris room before he boarded the plane to Stockholm in order to accept the Nobel Prize. The philosopher Alain saw in her by far the most gifted of his pupils. Among those for whom she sparkled as a star in the darkness of time were T. S. Eliot, Gabriel Marcel, Maurice Schumann, Dietrich von Hildebrandt. She was, and has remained until today, a rare jewel that it would be blasphemous to touch. The prestige of her death has shielded her from criticism. But difficult as such an attempt may be, it is high time to penetrate the overgrowth of legend and get to the person—because what she was and did fits all too well into a neo-irrationalist trend whose grim consequences cannot yet be foreseen.

The circumstances of her birth already contained those possibilities of her life and tragic dying that became reality. She was born in Paris in 1909. Social drama was bursting forth in a land that in its length and breadth was still yearning for a pastoral idyl. Jaurès was already at work. The waves of the Dreyfus case had hardly subsided. A young man named Léon Blum had just renounced his estheticism and allied himself with those who truly were still the damned of this earth.

Bernard Weil, her father, a respected and prosperous physician from an old Jewish-Alsatian family, was practicing in Paris. Salomea, her mother (also called Selma and "Mime"), was born in Rostov-on-Don and was of Austrian-Galician background. Thus does one become an outsider in the heart of France. Alsatians and Jews are never quite genuine *Français de France*. One bears a double taint when, in addition, the Alsatian element is mixed with the elusive Jewish element. It doesn't matter if you were born and grew up in the capital city a hundred times over. I agree for the most part with the Franco-Jewish author Paul Giniewski, who in a recently published book interprets Simone Weil's existence as having been essentially determined by her origins. One need only read her writings and the secondary literature alongside the memoirs of the one-year-older Simone de Beauvoir, and one immediately perceives a difference that reaches into existential depths. In the case of the indisputed "Française de France," Beauvoir, everything is natural, down to her exaggeratedly extreme leftist and feminist protest. In the case of the Jewess, born of Alsatian-Galician family, even what is seemingly most natural becomes problematic. The being of the one is credible whether you admire her or not; but even those who wildly overestimate the other will perforce have their doubts about her.

The least one can say is that Simone Weil was ill at ease with herself, and this state affected almost all who knew her. "I have the suspicion," T. S. Eliot wrote, "that Simone Weil was unbearable at times." In fact, she was unbearable not only "at times" but almost always and everywhere. A lyceum superintendent reproached her for the "diffuseness and confusion" of her courses—rightly, as is known. Her friend and host Gustave Thibon, for whom she wanted to work as a farmgirl (which, of course, miscarried, since she was of no help in either house or field), suffered from her presence, despite the respect he showed for her intelligence and her assiduous search for God. Her pupils were bored during her classes, which she conducted as passionately as she did monotonously, and the majority of them failed the final examination. At the grape harvest, in which she felt compelled to participate in order to experience the living conditions of the rural proletariat, she plagued a fellow worker with the wisdom of the Upanishads—something the girl sufferingly endured. Her most important work to my mind bears the title *The Need for Roots*. But she herself was unable to take root, either among her colleagues at the Ecole Normale Supérieure, or as a teacher, or as a factory worker and syndicalist. As a Jew, as a homely girl (who almost ingeniously made herself even more unattractive than she already was through sloppy dress and a messy hairdo), as a poor teacher and hopelessly inept worker, she forever stood "outside," before the gates, hungering. The God after whom she yearned also held her at a distance.

Three characteristics determined the existence of this extraordinary woman: her uncanny, penetrating intelligence, her fierce determination to cleanse mankind of its earthly smut, and a boundless longing to suffer. Having grown up with a brother three years her senior, who early in life was already regarded as a scientific genius, she competed with him; and while she didn't catch up with him, she reached the point where she could understand quantum physics and even write on this most difficult subject. Her knowledge of ancient languages, particularly Greek, far exceeded the requirements of the Ecole Normale Supérieure, which in themselves were already excessively demanding. When she immersed herself in East Asian wisdom, she studied Sanskrit. After her turn to Catholicism she acquainted herself so thoroughly with the field of theology that she was able to discuss the problems of patrology and scholasticism with any scholar.

Her intelligence was also strikingly Jewish. Contrary to a widespread belief, Jews are very often very stupid. At the same time, however, they are endowed as a group with a store of talent that causes embarrassment even to a philosemite. For if he enumerates the Jewish geniuses, even against his own will the ugly word "egghead" will occur to him. Less would be better, one thinks when reading Simone Weil. Even in her *Letter to a Priest*, which ostentatiously places *humility* at the core of all thought, she argues—against herself—in a hairsplitting manner that not only a malicious antisemite would characterize as "talmudic."

Also her passion for social reform went to the very extreme and even beyond. She saw social misery more clearly than others; the social injustice in France, which was alleviated only under Léon Blum's shortlived Popular Front, hurt her more than any of her contemporaries. But her reactions were far removed from both meliorist naïveté and rational-revolutionary methodology. Her social involvement, with all its estimable humaneness, brought nothing but trouble for her and burdens for her fellow fighters. In 1932 she took part in a strike in Le Puy; she managed to get arrested but had to go without the martyrdom to which she aspired—since the philosophy teacher was viewed as a harmless fool and immediately set free. Half in jest and half in scorn, she was called "la vierge rouge." During a miners' strike in Saint-Etienne she carried the red flag, a Joan of Arc without her Dunois and La Hire. But when she met Leo Trotsky shortly thereafter in her parents' home, he had the impression that she was a distraught person. He later remarked in a letter that it was hardly worth discussing her.

Precisely this "blind" involvement, as it were, contributed to the creation of the legend. Or had she really been a pioneer: in her criticism of the Soviet Union and the Comintern as well as in her anarcho-syndicalist rebellion? Was she a forerunner of those who today see salvation only in the economic self-management by the workers? Was she the presaging prophetess of the "nouveaux philosophes," who see everywhere only the "prince," the "maitre," and take the side of the plebs, whom all of the organized parties had arrogantly overlooked? She was, and then again she was not. For there exist texts, written by her in English exile, that bear witness to a frightening tendency toward authoritarian social systems of class character.

Actually, she was unpolitical. She saw in society, *every* society, only Plato's "Great Beast." She was always concerned only with pursuing her own salvation. No, not even that, but rather her own disaster; and at this, to be sure, she succeeded tragically. Wherewith we have touched the heart of her biography, her passion of passions. *She wanted to suffer*, absolutely and at any cost, even if she caused others pain by it—above all her parents, who were constantly fearful for her. She nourished herself poorly, wore garments of haircloth like a penitent, renounced a portion of her teacher's pay for the benefit of the unions, and finally died of hunger in England because she wanted to eat no more than the amount allotted in France to the "normal consumers," who had been placed on miserable rations—though, of course, even the poorest in that country naturally increased his food supply with illegal purchases. Was she a "masochist," as has often been said? That is a question of terminology. I prefer to apply the term only to a definite sexual deviation and would rather speak of her *self-torment*. Her Lord's Prayer would logically have had to end with the words: Forgive me never my debts and send me all that is bad, now and in the hour of my dying. Amen.

For years, since 1938 almost unceasingly, she suffered from agonizing headaches—Adrian Leverkühn's "head ache"—but I've never read that she ever submitted to serious medical treatment or even took analgesics. And above all: she imposed on herself the obligation to do physical labor although she was about as fit for it as she was for ballet. That was heroic, no doubt, even if here too a few remarks that will diminish the Simone Weil myth are imperative. Her work— first in a factory, then on a farm—lasted altogether a total of a half-year. Because she apparently wanted it that way, she was an *échec*, a failure: as a teacher, revolutionary, and worker. Even as a Christian.

Her Christianity, Manichean to the point of heresy, was nothing but suffering for God, and not salvation. What Weilian theology was, she herself described roughly in an opaque reflection on philosophy; in her work *La Connaissance surnaturelle*, whose very title contains an unresolvable contradiction, she wrote: "The characteristic method of philosophy consists in comprehending the problems as insoluble and in observing them, for years without end, expectantly, without any hope." Just as she denied herself sensible nourishment and modest everyday pleasures, she also denied herself every kind of intellectually positive accomplishment. The passionate Christian, who reminds us of Kierkegaard, also did not permit herself baptism, partly because she did not deem herself worthy of the sacraments, partly because she saw in the church less the mystical body of Christ than the *ecclesia triumphans* with its potential evil. Constantly in search of "perfect purity, perfect beauty, perfect justice," but aware that they are unattainable, she lost sight of all real beauty, good, and justice (since they can, after all, never be perfect). She was indeed "not of this world."

Her theological Manicheanism, whose roots we can explain only on the basis of her psychic constitution, extended deep even into her writing on completely profane subjects. In her notes on the "condition ouvriére," she penned very clever though not exactly overwhelmingly new thoughts on the alienation of female assembly-line workers. What she left out—because she hadn't experienced it—were the tiny compensations that enabled her fellow workers to endure: the fun of the Saturday dance, the short chat during work breaks, their love affairs. She herself, God's bride, was so chaste—and surely not only because her disposition and mournfully Jewish intellectual's face did not exactly attract droves of suitors—that she felt revulsion at any sort of physically tender communication. She regarded herself as a discard, a "slave," as she literally wrote. But absurdly, at the same time, as a genius of the absolute. To the extent that Simone Weil was really a clinical "case" (a thesis that can be confirmed), her condition would have to be diagnosed as that of an autodestructive megalomaniac. "Whatever I do," she wrote in *La Connaissance surnaturelle*, "I know with perfect clarity that it is not the Good. For what I do cannot be the Good once I do it. . . . Whatever one does, one accomplishes the Bad, and it is the unbearably Bad." Thus she proceeds from "I" to "one": Whenever she castigates her lamentable self she is carrying out morbid autodestruction; as soon as she says "one" and thus also includes others, she is setting herself up as a judge of mankind altogether, she is deifying herself. Delusions of personal insignificance and of grandeur become absurdly congruent.

If the concept of the absurd, in the theological and philosophical sense, can be used at all, it hardly applies to anyone as accurately as to Simone Weil. Absurd were not only her unsuccessful teaching career, her attempt to force her way into the world of labor, her search for the undiscoverable God; her conduct during the storms of the epoch was also absurd. She was a radical pacifist at a time when even a child could see that what mattered was to destroy Hitler and his ignominious empire at any price. She protested, by the way, in an extraordinarily and admirably bold letter to the Commissioner of Jewish Affairs of the Vichy regime, Xavier Vallat—but not as the Jew she was and as which the others designated her and had already sentenced her; rather she protested by referring to the fact that she had never visited a synagogue and that she was rooted in Hellenistic Christian culture—an argument that, given the historical moment, was both heroic and naïve. *A la fin du compte,* after she had tossed her pacifism overboard after all and had become a determined patriot, she wished to remain in France. But in June 1942, at the last moment, she emigrated with her parents to America, not in order to stay there, however, but rather in order to get to England and from there to return to France, a little detour she could have reasonably spared herself. But what did reason mean to her? "God created us free and intelligent so that we can give up our will and our intelligence . . ." (*The Notebooks of Simone Weil,* II). Thus she actually did offer up reason and life on the sacrificial altar of her God. In the process, she often had "more luck than brains," as the saying goes: The officials regarded her as an uninteresting case! Misfortune and martyrdom refused to materialize, even when one day, through pure clumsiness, she dropped a suitcase with Résistance documents, which then lay scattered on the street.

She was also an "uninteresting case" for the Free French Forces in London, where she had gone from America. Thanks above all to her friend Maurice Schumann, they barely let her have her way but never at all considered assigning her real tasks. *How* important for her the actual battle really was, is a question that must be asked. By this time she had long since given up her belief in the antifascist struggle as well as in the revolution, the hope of all those who, espousing the motto of the clandestine newspaper *Combat,* said: *De la résistance à la révolution!*

"Marx declared that religion is the opium of the people," she wrote. "No, the revolution is opium. The revolutionary hopes are a stimulant. All final systems are utterly wrong." We know that there is truth in this pronouncement. But obviously, it could only be half-true, since it was written at a time when the antifascist struggle possessed at least a *relative* finality. However, she was not interested in the world, but in God.

The conversion of this Jewess, who had grown up in a free-thinking milieu, had begun in 1938 while she was listening to a Gregorian mass at an Easter service; during this mystical experience the convert suffered from raging headaches. This moment of suffering determined the five next years still granted her. Her posthumous writings, especially *Waiting for God* and *Letter to a Priest* (addressed to the Dominican priest Perrin), lend both moving and dismaying testimony to the long passion of these years. The process of her detachment from reality can be followed like a case history, and the subtlest theological interpretations—the analogy with gnosis, with St. Theresa of Avila and Pascal—change next to nothing. Simone Weil shirked not only the demand of the day, not only common sense, but logic in general, which is the reflection of existence. Christ did not become her "favorite dish," as Heine puts it with revealing cynicism, but he did become the oxygen of her mental respiration. She didn't argue; instead she contented herself with brusque claims such as this: "Only the presence of Christ can explain the phenomenon of thoughts or supernatural acts, of justice, the comprehension of misfortune, of benevolence, altruism. To believe that they can be present where Christ is absent is godless, even blasphemous." Thus, there can be no salvation in this world. Not with God; for he can only be eternally awaited—in vain; but he cannot be reached through patient approximation. Utopia is a sacrilege. There remains only a sacrificial death.

Simone Weil died in an English hospital on August 24, 1943, according to the coroner from "heart failure due to myocardial insufficiency caused by hunger and pulmonary tuberculosis." His down-to-earth business did not permit him to say: "Suicide resulting from a religious compulsion neurosis."

Her essential writings appeared after her death, which, as the end of a national martyr, silenced the beginnings of any criticism in France. The shadow of death became a halo, and this not only in her own country but in the entire world. Thus it would have been in bad taste or, worse, blasphemy to disparage the unsystematic nature of her oeuvre. For who could demand of a mystic, chosen to suffer, that she systematize her experience of God like some academic theologian or other? One dared even less to examine her political statements. After all, she had carried the red flag at strikes, had been in Spain, wanted to risk her life for the Résistance. That sufficed in those days. Today it does not; for as Voltaire says: "One owes consideration to the living, to the dead only the truth."

Simone Weil *lived*, beyond her earthly sojourn, in the early post-war years. Only now is she, the deceased, truly dead, and truth is attaining its full due. From the incense that surrounded her there now emerges quite a bit that does not show up so well at all in full light, especially since it oddly forebodes what is being proposed in our own time by a Left that has become estranged from itself. The spirit of the estates, *"l'esprit des corporations,"* must be reawakened, we read in *The Need for Roots*. In those days that was the influence of Pétain's "révolution nationale." In a liberated France, she said, the great industrial complexes would be dissolved. Small manufactories, archaic in character and strewn far across the land, were to nourish and also clothe the nation as productive resources and capital goods. That too was Vichy, and since then the Left has probably abandoned itself a hundred times over to similar notions of a retrogressive utopia. While work—manual, but above all agricultural work—is to be limited in time, it is to have a quasi-sacred character. Is this the surmounting of alienation, or is it reactionary homesickness for something historically outmoded? The latter, naturally; not the former. "If the young worker thinks of settling down," she writes, "he would then be ready to take root."

In the dry fields of human reason there grows no nature cure for such revelations. In any case, let all those civilization-weary hyperintellectuals who project their personal nausea into the social sphere be warned of an influence that can produce no good. One can love Simone Weil the human being. One certainly must pity her. But Weil the thinker is of no concern to anyone who cares about the enlightenment of mankind.

Sartre
Greatness and Failure

IN HIS SARTRE biography, which recently appeared in France—the only one to date that truly merits the designation biography—the author, Francis Jeanson, calls his hero the "greatest philosopher of this century." One must be careful with such judgments. For nearly three decades I myself shared Jeanson's view: for me Jean-Paul Sartre was always the *primus inter pares*. Until this day I have not essentially revised my opinion. But in the course of the years, and especially the last five, it has become evident to me that Sartre's greatness did not exclude his failure, indeed that it perhaps consists in this very failure.

Two facts made me clearly aware of this: for one, Sartre's public declaration that also on the second ballot of the year in the French presidential election he would not vote for Mitterand, the candidate of the united French Left, since the entire election was a bourgeois fraud that an authentic revolutionary could only ignore; and second, there was my reading of the third volume of Sartre's work on Flaubert, a book that shows the now seventy-year-old philosopher in full command of his penetrating intelligence and visionary power. On the one hand, then, almost childishly spiteful political airs that are positively

"Sartre: Grösse und Scheitern," *Merkur* XXVIII (December 1974), 1123–37.

blind to reality, and, on the other hand, unimpaired genius. Greatness and failure. But was not this man destined to fail from the very beginning? Was not this failure an integral part of his philosophical thinking? Was he not condemned to failure by his concept of "dépassement," constant inner self-transcendence, permanent intellectual revolution against his own self? Was he not sentenced not only to freedom, as he often explained, but also to self-destruction? And it should be noted that the idea of "sentencing" already contains the unfreedom that Sartre always wanted to escape, at the price of what one commonly calls a "fulfilled and well-rounded life." Is the existence that must antecede essence, "ex-sistere" in the true sense of the word, as an emerging and an emerging from one's self, by definition not already self-destruction and thus failure?

With incomparable consistency, Sartre chose himself, discovered himself ever anew throughout his entire life. Perhaps this is demonstrated most strikingly in his autobiographical book *The Words*, in which he conjured up his childhood and mercilessly liquidated it at the same time. Where others dreamily search with their soul for the wonderland of childhood, Sartre viewed this land with the keen, rational eyes of a man without illusions. This permanent revolt lasted until the moment in which, for the sake of an entirely new political-moral rigorism, Sartre so to speak nihilated the alleged "political realism" that marked his activities from about 1953 to 1968 and found its expression in his more or less friendly attitude toward France's Communist Party.

Sartre became well known after the liberation of France in the year 1944–45. Although his great narrative *Nausea* had already appeared before the war and he had succeeded in having his drama *The Flies* performed during the war, it was only after the darkness of the German occupation had been lifted that he became the person he was to remain for many years. As though it were yesterday, I still see him before me as he was when I attended one of his lectures in Brussels in 1945: In those days the very small man appeared strong, even burly; reading from his book *What is Literature?* he made an overwhelming impression on all of us. And *what* he said—well, it was exactly what the hour demanded. And this brings me to the striking phenomenon of Sartre's fascination, of his astonishing success, which even had a popular dimension, and finally to the Sartre vogue. What was behind all that?

One can provide an answer and comprehend it only if one tries to picture the historical situation in the Western European countries that were occupied during the war and liberated in 1945. Fascism, so it seemed and so people wished to believe, was defeated. The old world, the one that had given birth to the economic crisis and fascism, was destroyed. Not only in Germany but also in the neighboring countries to the west, people thoroughly felt themselves to be children of "hour zero." A new day, a new start, a new order seemed to be called for. With an enthusiasm that was accompanied by the background music of rediscovered American jazz, poor but conscious of their triumph, people believed that the millennium was dawning. They made a clean slate of the past. Only the future mattered anymore. The middle class, which in dread of the Bolsheviks had gambled politically on Pétain and intellectually on the most wretched traditionalism, had become ridiculous in the consciousness of the nation. Even de Gaulle, on returning from exile, asked this middle class on the occasion of a meeting with big businessmen: "Where were you, gentlemen, while we were fighting?"

"De la Résistance à la Révolution" was not only the motto of the daily paper *Combat*, which had been edited by Camus during the underground period and was now appearing openly; it was the motto of the nation. Or so it seemed. For already the forces of yesterday were assembling. They pretended modesty, but they were aspiring tenaciously after their renascence. However, they kept out of sight, and it was the men and women of the start into the future who lifted their voices. The epoch was ripe for a new teaching. And what could accord better with the spirit of those days than Sartre's message of existence, of being sentenced to freedom, of anguish and its overcoming through man's active self-design—a message that was written and proclaimed with great suggestive power? He pointed this philosophy in two directions, above all toward the future, which for Sartre was always the true human dimension and has remained so until today. To this extent, his philosophy was in keeping with the dawn that people believed was in sight. But it also pointed to the past, although not that of the Third Republic. Rather it philosophically justified the Résistance *post eventum*. For it was in resistance that man had constantly been faced with choice and the risk of freedom—in this case a deadly one—that is inherent in it.

Only in the light of this duality—the pointing into the future and clarifying the situation of the immediate past—can the unprecedented success of Sartre's philosophy be understood. But one must ask oneself whether the politically aware French of this time were all philosophers. Were they able to read *Being and Nothingness*, Sartre's exceedingly difficult major work, which had already appeared during the war and demanded considerably specialized background knowledge and utmost concentration? Naturally not. Nor had they read it. The overwhelming majority of Sartre followers know his philosophy only from popularizing magazine articles, or at best from the lecture "Existentialism," which appeared in pamphlet form. Not to speak of the countless wildly dressed young people whom the burghers called "les éxistentialistes" and who populated the bars and cellar spots of Saint-Germaine-des-Prés; they were hardly concerned with Sartre's philosophy—had at most read *Nausea*, whose overall nihilistic tone gave them a pleasantly creepy feeling. What was regarded in Paris between the years 1945 and 1947 as existentialism was not least a phenomenon of fashion, a shortlived "craze," as the Americans term such mass moods. But existentialism was there in any case and spread from France into the world. Its spokesman, Jean-Paul Sartre, became an object of interest not only for the intellectuals but also for the crowd that delights in gossip. Sartre himself—who led not exactly a monastic life but, above all, one of hard work that often reached furious intensity—had nothing to do with the manifestations of fashion. Who was he? Only few knew at that time. Today we are better informed. The course of his life and thought lies clearly drawn before us. We need only to follow its lines.

"Part burgher-scare, part scared burgher": the description that Robert Neumann had once applied parodistically to Erich Kästner in Germany can to a degree certainly be applied to Sartre. Burgher-scare: that he is even today as an old man, when he becomes involved with the tiny and noisy Left at the farthest end of the radical scale. And a scared burgher, that applies too. For the aging and ailing Sartre, who is presently completing his *Flaubert* and is thus a scholar, has by no means been able to overcome entirely the middle-class mentality of his origins. This has always frightened him. He has suffered considerably from it and even his *Flaubert*, which contains hidden autobiographical elements, is a reckoning with his own middle-classness.

We know his early childhood from the book *The Words*, one of the very few works by Sartre that is available to us in an excellent German translation (thanks to Hans Mayer). There was his grandfather, Charles Schweitzer: larger than life, a Jupiter figure, related to the famous Albert and the later World Bank president, Pierre. He was an Alsatian of pronounced French patriotic convictions, a Germanist and German-hater, truly a figure from a novel. He cast his shadow on every member of the family: on his daughter, Anne-Marie, Sartre's mother, who had become a widow shortly after the boy's birth; on his wife, who was ever lost in her fantasies; on the child, whom he wished to form after his own image. The boy himself was obedient to the point of total submissiveness, precocious in an apparently quite charming manner, the pet of his early widowed mother, who already saw the man in the little fellow. When, decades later, Anne-Marie Mancy, née Schweitzer, the widowed Madame Sartre, outfitted a studio in her apartment for her already world-famous son, she said, according to Simone de Beauvoir: "I have the feeling as if this were my third marriage." For just when the boy was standing on the threshold of puberty, the young woman, whom early photos show to be very pretty, had the chance to marry a second time. The little naval officer Sartre, whose bride she had become as a mere child and who had died in a hurry, was forgotten. A new husband appeared, and for Jean-Paul, the little "poulou," as he was called, a *stepfather*.

Sartre remained strangely discreet about the period he spent in La Rochelle, where Monsieur Mancy held a high position with the port authority and thus was one of those notables whom Sartre later referred to as "salauds." Simone de Beauvoir, too, has told us nothing about this epoch. Even Francis Jeanson, his loyal pupil and biographer, communicates little of substance to us. Thus one has a certain right to speculate. It must have been a very difficult time for the boy, who until then had been married, as it were, to his youthful mother. Traces of this intermezzo can be found in Sartre's Baudelaire study and no doubt also in his masterful novelistic phenomenology of fascism, *The Childhood of a Leader*. Beyond that, however, one is left to conjecture about this decisive period in Sartre's life. As far as one can gather from the scant information, the engineer Mancy, a typical burgher, had no understanding for the boy's literary inclinations, which were already evident at that time. Nor could he have been indulgent toward a stepchild and tolerated the fact that the obedient and quite conformist little fellow that Sartre had been in his grandfather's house was turning into a little wild animal. His mother, always the wife, and this time the wife of a real husband, subordinated herself to the latter, and Poulou was made to feel it. I am firmly convinced that the origin of Sartre's furious hate for the bourgeoisie lies in just this period, of which we know so little. "The end is the truth of the beginning," he once wrote. And if we regard his late political behavior, which strayed more and more into eccentricity, as the end, then it is the truth of his beginning in La Rochelle.

Soon the tension dissolved, at least outwardly. Sartre first went to the lyceum in Paris as a resident pupil. After successful conclusion of middle school, he entered the famous Ecole Normale Supérieure. In the photos from this time we see a little gentleman with serious eyes, carefully parted hair, and a well-sitting necktie held by a tiepin. Simone de Beauvoir, who was just getting to know him at the Ecole Normale Supérieure, describes him differently in Alexander Astruc's Sartre film. He caught her attention, she said, for he was "neglected, dirty, and, in addition to all that, constantly after the girls." I would add that this last-mentioned characteristic is an extremely likable one. And Sartre does not disavow it even today. In this film we hear from his own mouth that he prefers the company of women to that of men. And, of course, these women ought to be pretty.

Thus, from early on Sartre was neither the stay-at-home he has been described as here and there, nor the model pupil, nor, naturally, a daydreaming loner. On the contrary, he was constantly surrounded by friends. One of them was Raymond Aron, later his most "intimate enemy," if it may be put that way, a philosopher who subsequently converted to a resolute conservatism and yet continues to define himself in relation to Sartre. Another was the writer Paul Nizan, a Communist Party member who after the Molotov-Ribbentrop pact quit the party and was killed at Dunkirk in 1940. And above all there was Simone de Beauvoir, with whom the young Sartre was already then beginning his lifelong adventure. I mean by that the sheer daredevil and, in this case, singularly successful attempt at a full partnership with the total freedom of both individuals. We must picture the life of the highly gifted philosophy student and later professor of philosophy at the lyceums of Laon and Le Havre as an extremely rich life, rich in intellectual as well as sensual matters. We can discover only one area where it was almost woefully lacking: the area of politics. Yes, practically until the start of the war, Sartre was an essentially nonpolitical person. His later political activity, which swept him into the machinery of society and drew him into contradictions and finally absurdities, is comprehensible only in the light of the young Sartre's nonpolitical attitude—for which the mature man never forgave himself. In later periods of his life, he wanted, at a furious pace, to make up for what he had neglected as a young man, at an age when political consciousness is normally formed. His vague sympathies for the French Popular Front of 1936 did not manifest themselves decisively, or, as the later Sartre put it so often that the word already sounds quite worn today, they did not became *engagement*.

Most striking in this regard is the almost incomprehensible indifference of the young Sartre, who in 1934 lived for a time in Berlin as a scholar of the Institut Français. Just try to imagine: Here was a young man who had set out to discover Germany, but what he found were not the bestial deeds of fascism that already then were becoming fully evident, not the persecution of liberal politicians and Jews, not the rotten vapors of Nazi pseudo-intellect, but rather: Husserl and Heidegger. These experiences were important enough. But for Sartre, they did not exist in a political context at all. The Sartre who did *not* see ordinary and absolutely clear-cut fascism and that other Sartre, who today sees fascism everywhere and wants to tear the mask of bourgeois democracy from its face, complement one another. The latter is inexplicable without the knowledge of the former; the former already anticipated the latter.

So Sartre did not discover the Nazis in Berlin but instead Husserl and Heidegger. That meant practically nothing in the political field, but it had tremendous importance intellectually. For Sartre had been schooled in Cartesianism and sanctified "raison," and had read neither Hegel nor Marx thoroughly; for him Kierkegaard was merely a name that was connected to obscure reference points of a purely philosophical-historical character. And now he encountered something that was completely new to him: Husserl's transcendental *subject* and Heidegger's concept of *existence*. During this time, Sartre developed the trains of thought that he set down in his first major work, *Being and Nothingness*, which appeared in France in 1943. But here I would like to jump ahead in time. How can one compress into a few sentences what was both essential and essentially new in this voluminous and extremely difficult book? The undertaking—or, better, venture—is more than bold; but I cannot back off from it.

What Sartre is aiming at in *Being and Nothingness* and what he really succeeded in achieving—to the extent that one can speak at all of attainments and truths in the humanities—is the ontological substantiation of the subject in its struggle with the world of objects and with the others. The subject as the "for-itself" aspires to become the "in-itself," that is, to become object. Man must resist this aspiration or temptation if he is to be himself. As "he-himself," he may never be essence, however; rather he must always be existence, trusting that he is able to "make," to form himself and, by means of his inborn chance for freedom, to "nihilate" his essence as soon as it threatens to petrify into being, "être." And those things are "nihilated" by the free subject that cause the nightmare of being that is so grippingly described in the narrative *Nausea*. Here an ontologist was at work who was still indebted to subjective idealism, and the Marxists were not completely wrong when they later reproached the early Sartre for his philosophical idealism. For the loathing of being is nothing but the aversion to all that is thing, to the nature that is the object of scientific investigation. Toward it man affirms his subjectivity, which is his sole personal possession and which he must nonetheless destroy in permanent revolt.

However, this subject, which sovereignly experiences itself, is constantly threatened by the *Other*, the fellow man and his look. Sartre's pronouncement in *No Exit* has been quoted all too often and mostly in false context: "Hell—that is the others"—as though in his subjectivism the philosopher were also a solipsist. He is not one, as we shall see. But his phenomenology discovered a truth of living being that no one can escape because everyone has experienced it. The Other thwarts my design through his subjectivity. His freedom opposes mine. His look turns my absolute subject into object: I can be *seen*, as though I were a thing among things. The mere fact that the consciousness of the Other exists as his subjectivity, that I have no access to it, that it must forever be radically alien to me, plunges me from my for-itself into the inertia of the in-itself. Under the look of the Other I am made from an existence into an object, into being, into essence. Sartre calls the process of the thwarting of the subjectively active design "la chute originelle," the "ur-plunge" or "ur-fall."

This splendid phenomenology is still valid today, since it can be confirmed through experience at any time; but it ignores society. The Sartre who wrote *Being and Nothingness* knew nothing about social conditionalities. Only much later, in his *Critique of Dialectical Reason*, did he attempt to complete his phenomenology by means of social criticism. Colette Andry, one of the best Sartre scholars, was therefore correct in writing that while *Being and Nothingness* does precede *Critique of Dialectical Reason* chronologically, from a logical point of view the latter must be placed before the early work. For the subject will be able to live and unfold its subjectivity only under conditions of a free, nonalienating society.

It is a biographical fact that Sartre experienced society first as a soldier and then as a prisoner of war. The third volume of the novel cycle *The Roads to Freedom*, which has unfortunately remained incomplete, tells us how the "demi-hero" of the work, Mathieu Delarue, in the midst of his comrades, who are being transported in a cattle car from defeated France to Germany, suddenly experiences himself as an integral part of a community. From the time of his war imprisonment, from which, by the way, he was already released in 1941, Sartre's existence has been a *social* existence and, no matter how rigorously he would deny it if someone said it to him, also a *national* existence.

Today one can hardly picture the dreariness of the German-occupied Paris to which Sartre returned in order to resume a position as lyceum teacher. Collaborators, morally inferior types—some of whom may also have been gifted writers, such as Brasillach, Drieu la Rochelle, and Céline—dominated the scene, along with black marketeers. The ruling class was wallowing in a resignation that was both masochistic and, since it was finally freed of the nightmare of communism, not particularly burdensome. It was also lightened by the knowledge that they, the ruling class, would always have enough to eat. The *misera plebs* didn't count any longer, and the occupiers had put an end to the tricks of the corruptive Jews. For a man like Sartre and his companion, Simone de Beauvoir, the call to resistance was irrefusable.

And with this we rudely touch the great man's Achilles' heel. Naturally, he was ready to resist. But basically it all remained latent. The founding of an illegal group, "Freedom and Socialism," was an abortive undertaking that became little more than an intellectual debating club. Sartre didn't find the right connections. A visit to André Malraux came to nothing because the famous author maintained a politely reserved distance. No doubt, the former fighter pilot in the Spanish Republican air force and later "Colonel Berger" of the Maquis

didn't put much stock in the military abilities of his undersized intellectual caller. During the occupation Sartre had a few certainly not
unhazardous contacts, especially toward the end of the war when he
belonged to the illegal national writers committee. But he was no
partisan, no saboteur, not even a regularly active distributor of revolutionary fliers. Here, too, there are obvious links to the present-day
Sartre. What he neglected back then, he wished to realize later. Revolutionary counterforce, which he had no chance dramatically to practice in the decisive years, later became his philosophy of violence. It is
detectable today in his revolutionary stand, which does not shirk from
excess and is leading him into the proximity of Maoist grouplets that
real-politically don't stand a chance.

I wish neither to criticize nor to belittle the most estimable intellectual radicalism with which he is destroying his own prestige for the
sake of the cause that he deems to be good and necessary. I am attempting to explain him psychologically, and I believe that my expli-
cation is not far off the mark. To recapitulate: We are dealing with a
man who awakened to political consciousness rather late. Before the
war his aversion to the bourgeoisie had manifested itself only in his
provocation of the outward form of bourgeois life. Late political awakening and hatred for the bourgeoisie that finally discovered its ideological superstructure and its analytical justification, in the end produced
the Sartre we know today: a writer who, in accordance with his philosophy, not only ceaselessly transcends himself and his social station,
but beyond that passionately demolishes them pure and simple.
Therein lies his greatness. Therein lies his failure. For politics is and
remains the art of the possible; and that "extension of the field of
possibilities" that Sartre so urgently demanded during the fateful
French May of 1968 is limited by reality. Today, incidentally, he says
of himself that he is no longer a realist. Had he ever been one? At least
he attempted to be one. And with this we return to his political development.

As we have seen, Jean-Paul Sartre was the man of a resistance that
did not fully attain to manifestation; later he became the philosophical
defender of the Résistance. His play *The Flies* is part of what he understood to be his Résistance activity. It is perhaps his most noteworthy
play and was performed in Paris during the occupation. To be sure,
this performance had a somewhat ambiguous character. Certainly:

Orestes, who appears on the scene as a self-willed avenger and murders Aegisthus, can be seen as a resistance fighter; one can interpret his deed as an act of resistance and a summons. Nonetheless, we cannot entirely ignore Malraux's later reproach, when he was already de Gaulle's minister, that during the occupation and without challenging the Germans directly, Sartre permitted a play to be performed at all. Would not total abstinence have been more appropriate at that time? I don't know and cannot presume a judgment. There are good arguments for both stands: for the one that consisted in shunning the entire cultural enterprise, which was ultimately dependent on the occupiers; and for the other, which maintained that one had to utilize every opportunity for public activity in order to serve the cause. This much is certain: When France was liberated and the revolution that people were longing for as the natural continuation of the Résistance appeared to be the order of the day, Sartre was not entirely in agreement with his past.

He was at the height of his fame when his quarrel with the communists began; it had many turning points and lasted for years. At first, in the days, months, and years of the period between 1944 and 1947, the fronts were clearly drawn. Above all, it was the communists who drew them. They saw a danger in Sartre and his success. The party ideologues polemicized against him as a "petty-bourgeois, idealistic" divider of the proletariat. At a congress of intellectuals in Wroclaw, arranged by the communists, the Soviet author Fedayev called Sartre a "writing hyena." For his part, our philosopher had seen through the dogmatism and Stalinist barbarity. He, the existentialist and proclaimer of subjective freedom, could not accept what he termed still long afterward in *Critique of Dialectical Reason* the "inhuman anthropology" of Soviet-oriented communism. The communists let fly at him, and he was not one to take their blows lying down. He polemicized against the Stalinists, and not only in the monthly *Les Temps Modernes*, which he created and which is still under his patronage. As late as 1948 he wrote the play *Dirty Hands*, which is most critical of communism. And he went even a step further. In 1948, together with a number of unaffiliated leftists, among them especially David Rousset, the author of one of the few concentration-camp books that does justice to its appalling subject, he founded the RDR ("Rassemblement Démocratique Révolutionaire"), which intended to be an assembly of all leftist-revolutionary forces, free of Stalinist dogmatism. The undertaking had to fail, not only because the few intellectuals who had designed it found no contact with the people, but above all because at this time the Cold War broke out in all its fury and clearly allowed only the alternative of siding with the USA as the leading power of a world that called itself the "free" world, or to do battle for communism in domestic and foreign politics in the shadow of the Soviet Union. Sartre chose his stand at the side of the CPF—but that only became clear in the early fifties.

In the meantime, he had read Marx thoroughly and was intellectually equipped. Not that he would have become an outright Marxist like the representatives of the DIAMAT; he did not give up his existentialism, or let us perhaps better say: the *subject*. We can term the stand that he was to assume thenceforth for a long time, and that he has basically maintained, existential Marxism. What also did not come into question for him was membership in the party. He always valued too highly his independence, his freedom from all institutionalism, if you wish, his consciously chosen position as an outsider that later caused him to refuse even the Nobel Prize. His deliberations, which he had set down theoretically in the essay "The Communists and Peace" (1953), were approximately these: Democratic-revolutionary movements with no backing among the workers are hopeless and ahistorical. Whether one likes it or not, the Communist Party of France is the representative of the proletariat, which is in turn the rising class, with a future in history. To make enemies of the communists would have meant for him at that time foregoing the realization of his engagement, and he wanted by all means to revise his youth as a "nonpolitical man" and to achieve effect with his writing.

Today he calls the time of his marching-in-step with the communists his "realism," from which he wishes to disassociate himself for the sake of a more decisive, morally rigorous position that he sees best embodied in the young French Mao followers—although he is not really a Maoist himself. The communists, in their realism or their Realpolitik—and in French one uses the German word "la Realpolitik" when one means opportunism—became in his eyes a reformist party, part of the system that was to be overcome, an "opposition respecteuse," as he likes to call it, in allusion to his play *The Respectable Prostitute*.

One must not imagine Sartre's association with the communists as a cozy family idyl. On the contrary, it was a quite agitated household in which he was living, constantly stirring with quarrel and vexation. There was no lack of crises. His numerous journeys to the Soviet Union were not pleasure trips. On one of them, Khrushchev, influenced by the then French CP secretary, Maurice Thorez, treated Sartre with a coldness that exceeded all reasonable limits. Sartre never believed blindly. Quite the opposite, with open eyes and without illusions he wanted to experience the reality of communism and still not revoke his treaty of friendship with it. His motto was: "Do not allow yourself to be cut off from the communists under the influence of global Cold War trends inspired by America." He recalled all too well the collapse of the "Rassemblement Démocratique Révolutionaire," which his coworker in the movement, David Rousset, had wanted to bring into the American camp. Later he found his way out of the situation, which he already felt to be a dilemma at that time. But it is clear enough today that it was a way that led nowhere. For with his turn to Maoism, or to the New Left, which was playing at anarchism, Sartre rejected not only "la Realpolitik" but political reality altogether.

The first crisis between Sartre and his communist friend-foes broke out in 1956, when Soviet tanks were putting a quick end to the Hungarian uprising. It could be resolved, because at that time it was actually possible for a man of the Left to tell himself that without the Soviet intervention in Hungary, not the social democracy of a Nagy would have triumphed but rather the White terror. The total break did not occur until twelve years later. Prague, August 1968, signaled the end of an association that at bottom had always been intellectually perverse. But we still haven't reached that point. We are concerned with the Sartre who in the fifties did not want to break with the communists, whom he saw as the legitimate spokesmen of the proletariat and therewith as the bearers of the future. But one must also consider this: If in political practice, in his battle against France's Indo-China war, his "no" to American claims to world hegemony, his decisive "yes" to the national revolution of the Algerians, Sartre sided with the communists, he nevertheless accomplished a task in the theoretical field that was entirely fit to deal orthodox communism of the Moscow stamp a mortal blow. He was writing his second major work, *Critique of Dialectical Reason*, which was intended as a paraphrase on the theme of Marxism but in truth outlined a wholly new and, as I believe, trans-Marxist anthropology. The work appeared in French in 1960. Until today, apart from Raymond Aron's extensive exposition, it has not been received in France as it deserves (not to speak of Germany, where it appeared in 1967). No doubt, it will take years before this work—along with Sartre's *Flaubert*—finds its readers and then perhaps confirms what Francis Jeanson has said in his biography of his teacher: that this man was the greatest philosopher of the century.

A word about the *man* Sartre may perhaps be appropriate at just this point. For in 1960 he had become fifty-five years old. That is more than the "âge de raison" he described in *The Roads to Freedom*. Rather, it is already plain "l'âge," in any case, the beginning of aging. I have already alluded to the adventure of togetherness-in-freedom that he had begun as a young man with Simone de Beauvoir and that he is still living in an exemplary manner today. It is not necessary to discuss his affairs and hers, which never endangered the accord of two free spirits. That would be grossly indiscreet and moreover would add no new facets to our picture of Sartre.

The matter is different with the *worker* Sartre, whose image is obscured by fame and whose voice is drowned out by the fuss over his political acts. For here we have the rare example of a man who is possessed by work and at the same time, in the full sense of the innocent-sounding and yet so momentous verb, also *lives*. Sartre has almost never ceased working daily at his desk; except that his desk was not always a desk but frequently an improvised working space in some uncomfortable hotel room. For he worked tirelessly also on his numerous trips: to North Africa, Latin America, China, Central Europe, to the Soviet Union and its vassal states, and again and again to Italy—where until recently he spent his summers in Rome. On these trips he has always engaged in public events, in lectures and interviews, and in discussions that mostly lasted until late into the night. His way of life was and remained tremendously strenuous, the more so as there was always an inordinate amount of smoking and heavy drinking on these occasions. If he was exhausted, he swallowed up to twenty pep pills a day. Moreover—but this is a subject that requires a separate study—he had to struggle for years with the neuroses about which he wrote, as concealed autobiography, in his work on Flaubert and already earlier in *Saint Genet*.

In such circumstances of overexertion and a physical condition that was growing ever more precarious, Sartre wrote his *Critique of*

Dialectical Reason, which unfortunately can be discussed here only briefly (as was also true of *Being and Nothingness*). The book is concerned with a new foundation for Marxism, a new anthropology to be integrated into Marxism. If I were compelled to distill the essence of the work into a single sentence, I would say that in it Sartre reintroduced the *subject* into Marxism, or better: introduced it for the first time. To be sure, however, the individual here is no longer the same one who creates a self-design free of societal conditions. For Sartre this individual had been a bourgeois mystification. The burgher—in this instance, the burgher Sartre—had mistaken his particular middle-classness as universal. In *Critique of Dialectical Reason* the subject, which is socially atomized or serialized, as Sartre puts it, now realizes itself in the revolutionary group. It was a revolutionary group that captured the Bastille, and in it the individual no longer recognized the enemy in the Other but rather in himself.

In the group the subject no longer suffocates but, on the contrary, finally attains its potential. In the revolutionary act of the group the person's freedom is rescued from seriality, which is a new definition of alienation. In opposition to what Sartre calls the "inhuman anthropology" of Stalinism, an anthropology is drawn here in which the subject discovers itself and by the same act creates itself.

Published in 1960, *Critique of Dialectical Reason* was less noticed than all of Sartre's earlier works, partly because of its great difficulties, partly because at that time structuralism was celebrating its triumphs as philosophy and intellectual vogue. But then a historic event occurred that lent this book an unforeseen relevance: the May–June revolt of 1968, which missed becoming a revolution by a hair and in which the "groupe en fusion," seen by Sartre with visionary power, had manifested itself in revolutionary violence. The year 1968 was the great turning point for Jean-Paul Sartre. For it was not only the events in France that determined it. In August of that year the USSR, with its "tank communism," had overrun Czechoslovakia.

The break with communism that followed this event was both a negative and a positive occurrence in the life of the philosopher Sartre. It was positive inasmuch as he recognized at this time that the Soviet Union and the Western communist parties influenced by it had renounced the proletarian revolution and were simply practicing classical power politics; that is, a realism was asserting itself that looked very much like despairing opportunistic Realpolitik. It was negative in the sense that Sartre henceforth remained emotionally bound to the events of May and their undeniably grandiose atmosphere of revolutionary awakening, whose nature could almost be regarded as esthetic. But he not only disavowed communist Realpolitik, but—while in the process of writing his *Flaubert*, a highly elite book that is beyond the grasp of any worker—he allied himself ever closer with the extreme Left of Maoist persuasion, a Left that was situated in a political vacuum. He now surrounds himself with young people who address him familiarly with "tu," while he disconcertingly sticks to the formal "vous" in the company of old friends and even his mate, Simone de Beauvoir. He lends his voice and his prestige, or what has remained of it, to a few agitated young people who have no support in France, least of all among the workers. The antibourgeois disposition that he had dragged along from his early youth effected a grand accomplishment. I mean the philosophically momentous *Critique of Dialectical Reason*. But in the last few years, he has developed a senile obstinacy whose armor is impenetrable. And for all those who for a quarter-century saw in Sartre their teacher, it is a deeply disturbing and sad spectacle the way this man clings to notions of *absolute revolution* that can no longer be socially legitimized. He, whose most tremendous accomplishment was self-transcendence, thinking against himself, was unfaithful to himself for years as editor, until recently, of a wretched little paper that called itself *Liberation* and was consciously written in a miserable style; for everyone knows that refined language is one of the bourgeoisie's means of repression.

And yet the old Sartre is still with us. I am speaking of the author who, with the energy left him, is completing his *Flaubert*, a titanic project that attempts to join theoretically phenomenology, psychoanalysis, and Marxism; a work in which the neurosis that induced Flaubert's attacks of pseudo-epilepsy is related by the author to his own self and experienced by him, and at the same time is interpreted by the Marxist as the socially conditioned spiritual illness of the nineteenth-century bourgeois writer. This gigantic, autobiographically informed philosophical work of literary art is Sartre's greatest—of this I have no doubt.

The tragedy is only that Sartre is writing this book with a bad conscience. In interviews with French Maoists that have just appeared in book form, he said it himself: As the author of *Flaubert* he is the "classical intellectual" of bourgeois provenance who stands in contradiction to what he actually wished to be, the "new intellectual," who merges wholly with the people. The failure of Sartre's greatness does not lie in the fact that he has squandered his prestige as the intellectual representative of the nation; he wanted to relinquish it, he always scorned it, as he did the Academie Française, as he did the Nobel Prize. Sartre's shipwreck—and I venture this metaphor—is his alienation from reality, which has been growing ever more clear since 1968; it is his *false consciousness* in the true sense of the word.

Just as I was completing this essay I received word that Jean-Paul Sartre has petitioned the German judicial authorities for permission to discuss problems of revolution with Andreas Baader, the imprisoned member of the Baader-Meinhof group. The normal intellectual wonders, not without consternation, what in the world Sartre hopes to learn from Baader. How revolutions are *not* made, *cannot* be made in a country whose democracy is still functioning after all? Here, too, false consciousness. But at the same time, impressive consistency. Tout compte fait: greatness and failure.

Enlightenment as
Philosophia Perennis

WHAT HAPPENED THAT the Enlightenment became a relic of intellectual history, good enough at best for the diligent but sterile exertions of scholars? What sad aberration has brought us to the point where modern thinkers do not dare to employ concepts such as progress, humanization, and reason except within damning quotation marks?

The standard answers are close at hand; anyone can pass them on as the worn coins of a spirit that lost its own identity long ago. Enlightenment? A bourgeois mystification. Reason? The evil instrumentality of unjust, outdated forms of production. Humaneness? The pretext of the third estate, which presented its particular interests as universal values so that with their help it could exploit the fourth estate in good conscience. Progress? The frenzied obsession with production and profit of a bourgeoisie that has subjugated the proletarian and with him the earth. Thus, we late descendants of the great eighteenth and incomparable nineteenth centuries find ourselves in a world that is sick

"Aufklärung als Philosophia perennis," in *Über Jean Améry* (About Jean Améry; Stuttgart: Klett-Cotta, 1977), pp. 69–78. This essay is an address given by Améry on May 16, 1977, upon receiving the Hamburg Lessing Prize, an award created to honor the great German Enlightenment poet Gotthold Ephraim Lessing (1729–81).

with progress, impoverished, and suffocating in its own excrement. "The earth's ruin through the mind," as another Lessing, with the given name of Theodor, solemnly proclaimed.[1]

But I protest passionately and with all the energy at my disposal. Not that I would venture the absurd claim that the damages of civilization in the individual-humane and sociopolitical realms are only neurotic fantasies of a *malade imaginaire!* The author of the book *Lefeu oder Der Abbruch*, which contains the bitter expression "decay of the epoch in gloss," is free of illusions, of all naïve pleasure in the accomplishments of progress, which put to shame the discoveries of a humanely intended science.[2] And still, I profess loyalty to enlightenment, specifically to the *classical* enlightenment—as a *philosophia perennis* that contains all of its own correctives, so that it is an idle game dialectically to dissect it. I stand up for analytical reason and its language, which is logic. In spite of all that we have had to experience, I believe that even today, as in the days of the Encyclopedists, knowledge leads to recognition and recognition to morality. And I maintain that it was not the Enlightenment that failed, as we have been assured ever since the first wave of the romantic counterenlightenment, but rather those who were appointed its guardians.

I would like to state concretely what I mean, in the simplest possible way and without fearing in the least the accusation of being "banal." On the contrary and as an aside, so to speak: Nothing would be more beneficial for the trendy thinkers who on every occasion disguise the poverty of their thoughts with the pinchbeck of cheap "brilliance" than a good, bracing regimen of banality. The first consideration that I feel compelled to voice in this regard points to an evident fact: *All* of the freedoms we enjoy and are obliged to pass on are fruits of the bourgeois Enlightenment. Here we stand, critically minded intellectuals, and whatever intellectual freedom we possess, we owe to the Enlighteners: from Montesquieu to Freud, from Locke, Condorcet, and Diderot to Marx, Feuerbach, and Russell. Whatever insights we have acquired that have helped us to know ourselves and gain assurance in the world, we would not possess without the scientific world view of the Enlightenment. That applies to the little things of our daily life as well as to tremendous macro- and microphysical phenomena. Robert Musil once spoke in passing of our foolish arrogance toward science, saying that the "educated" do not know the name of the man who bestowed on the world the indescribable blessing of narcosis! We need only to go back for a moment to the condition of the world and the mind before the onset of the Enlightenment, and with horror we will perceive fear: fear of the unleashed powers of nature, fear of bodily pain, for which there was no relief, fear of the evil eye, of gods, idols, and demons, fear of the rulers whose sadistic exercise of power was not curbed by law, fear of one's own fear, which arose from the unconscious and made man the slave to his "id."

To be sure, it would be presumptuous to say that we are living without fear today. But if we compare our worst fears—of war and atomic disaster, of economic adversity—to mankind's fear and trembling in the pre-Enlightenment epochs, they appear like the coy heartache of a nineteenth-century patrician's daughter beside the raging hunger pangs of the Silesian weavers. Given such oppressively momentous facts, an enlightenment that seeks to transcend itself but in so doing destroys the foundations of rational-moral thought, is distressing. And it is against this that I intend to polemicize. Perhaps one can guess what I have in mind. Not the miserable, but relatively cozy, German irrationalism of the early twentieth century that Thomas Mann so incomparably rendered forever ridiculous in his description of the Kridwiss Circle in *Doctor Faustus*, not the "Conservative Revolution," then; not Klages, Spengler, Alfred Schuler, or Joseph Nadler, who constantly found it necessary to play off the "soul"—whatever that is!—against the "mind." I want to pick a quarrel neither with the vitalism of a Driesch, which is now ancient history, nor, in the name of Julien Benda, with Henri Bergson and his philosophy of the *élan vital*. Everything that Heinrich Mann once called "profound drivel" has already been left by the roadside of intellectual history. It would be a pure waste of energy if I were to present arguments here that would only be forcing wide-open doors. No, I do not have to defend the Enlightenment against "profound drivel." But the time has come to protest against a high-flown hogwash that decks out homey old irrationalism in a new set of chic clothes—Parisian chic, to be precise. No matter how closely I listen, no voice can be heard that calls out: the kings are naked. It is sheer high-flown hogwash of the most dangerous sort when Roland Barthes presumes to declare, in a pseudo-radical manner that just flabbergasts the up-to-date intellectuals, that language itself is fascist, as this gentleman did before a vacuously enraptured audience, of all things, on the occasion of his inaugural lecture at the Collège de France. It was unleashed sophisticated twaddle when already two years ago the philosopher Guilles Deleuze and the psychologist Félix Guattari in their *Anti-Oedipus* sought arguments against the skeptical, reasonable Freud from no other than Wilhelm Reich, in fact, the late Reich, whose clinical insanity is a demonstrated fact. It is unwieldy anti-Enlightenment chatter and nothing more when Michel Foucault disclaims the moral progress of criminal justice (which, alas, is proceeding at a snail's pace) by castigating the triste surveillance and sentencing practiced by modern jurisdiction more severely than he does the bestialities that were customary before the Enlightenment.

And what is one to say about the intentions of the anti-psychiatrists, for whom reason is nothing but bourgeois alienation of man, and who celebrate insanity as the free inner space of people who they claim are permanently manipulated by society? Subjectively, their intentions are good, that is certain; but objectively they are a menace to culture. What is one to say of thinkers like Roger Geraudy, who has already seen better days but—excommunicated from the Marxist-Orthodox church—damns enlightened civilization as eurocentric oppression and holds Black African initiation rites in higher esteem than the philosophy of the Peripatetics? Do not all these people, dazed by ideological "fog formations of the brain," see, hear, and feel that *they* are the negatively manipulated ones? That they are being manipulated by intellectual fashions that coming seasons will have forgotten as they do the latest models of haute couture? Doesn't it enter their minds that their irrationalism is serving the cause of the rulers, the publishers, the media czars, the newspapers concerned only with circulation figures just as effectively as once did the soulful outpourings of the Conservative Revolution? Of course not. On the contrary, they regard themselves as the real enlighteners, the appointed demystifiers, perhaps the prophets of a coming revolution.

If I am right, then France, forsaken by the sanity of Cartesianism, really is at present the center of an artfully dissembling anti-Enlightenment that does not see itself for what it is. It would be unjust, however, to blame only the French. In any event, German complicity must not be passed over in silence. The king's new clothes were worn in postwar Germany too, and very early at that. After many years I was again reading in *The Dialectics of the Enlightenment* by Adorno and Horkheimer, a book that had filled me with enthusiasm three decades ago; I declare without hesitation that fright and deep discomfort seized me on rereading this most brilliant work. In their effort to rescue the classical Enlightenment from the naïveté determined by its epoch and to develop it further dialectically, the authors let themselves be carried away and made horrendous claims that, taken literally, could serve as an alibi for the very worst kind of obscurantism. The book contains extremely disturbing declarations, such as these: "Enlightenment is totalitarian." "Enlightenment dissolves the injustice of the old inequality, direct imperium, but at the same time it perpetuates it through universal mediation, the relating of every existent to every other." "In the face of the Enlightenment concepts are like pensioners in the face of industrial trusts: no one is able to feel secure." "On the way from mythology to logistics, thinking lost the element of self-reflection, and today machinery cripples people even as it feeds them."

I know, I know, it is an intellectual sin to quote "sentences torn from their context," as it is said. But what I am citing are paradigmatic judgments. Every one of them contains resistance against logic, irrational rage against the technical-industrial world, the wholly false conception that the historical Enlightenment was nothing but the instrument of a brutal bourgeoisie that was securing its dominion. They are blind to the obvious historical fact that the bourgeois was also a *citoyen* at the same time, that in the particular nature of the bourgeois revolution there was *also* universality, that while industry and machines did harm the individual, they also freed him from the oppressiveness and dullness of the biblically accursed soil. I know the mountain peasants of the past in my native Austria, and I know the American farmer. No ever so refined dialectical philosophizing can rob me of the conviction that, thanks to his machines, the latter leads a life more worthy of a human being than did the former in bygone times.

And the mention of dialectical thinking gives me a cue. I have tried elsewhere to grapple with dialectics as a specific mannerism of thought. I rejected the methodological claim of dialectical philosophizing, but I acknowledged with admiration the inspiring strength of the dialectical process. One is not indebted to Sartre, as is the author of this text, without having tried one's hand at dialectics. There is not one of my writings, hardly a single sentence that I've written, in which traces of dialectics cannot be detected. And yet, when I try today, at a late date, to clarify for myself whether dialectics has brought the history of human thought more good or more bad, it seems to me as if the "Bacchic frenzy," as Hegel himself called the (dialectically) "true," in the last analysis created more vainglorious mischief than it did possibilities for authentic progress. I don't want to go as far as the philosopher Etiemble, who spoke of Hegel in a recently published text as the "architraitre," the "archtraitor" of reason. But to the same extent that I clarify for myself the puzzles, the distortions, and the acrobatics of dialectics that maliciously force reason, pure and practical, into the retirement home of intelligence, I become estranged from this manner of thinking. This happens all the more easily since I see in Marx today less the dialectician and successor to Hegel than the prophet of a *new morality*, the direct descendent of the very same bourgeois Enlightenment that in the eyes of modern Marxists—who wish to know nothing more of the human being—is but an unwieldy instrument of the ruling classes.

How lovely, spirited, and virile, how sensible and lucid the classical Enlightenment appears against the background of dialectical obfuscation. All this despite its naïveté and epistemological deficiency, despite its optimism, which is called "childish," although I believe that soon it will gloriously revive as the highest level of humane maturity. Together with the skepticism that does not contradict it but rather ingeniously complements it, the benevolent optimism of the Enlightenment, with its constant values of freedom, reason, justice, and truth is our *sole hope* of making history and in so doing of carrying on the one truly humane business: lending meaning to the meaningless. It is the intellectual and social demand of the day that we rediscover the classical Enlightenment. Certainly, the perspectives have shifted. We no longer believe that we know, as once did the Encyclopedists, but we know always—in scientific research as well as in the humanities—that we merely believe and that we must constantly be prepared to revise our scientific doctrines. Revision, moreover, is taking place all the time, and no one is more keenly aware of this than the natural scientists when, like the great Enlightener Jacques Monod, they recognize our presence here as the product of blind chance and yet, as Sartre says, create something out of that into which we have been made.

A little less than fifty years ago, Thomas Mann, the author who is dearest to me among all those writing in my native tongue, spoke on the 200th birthday of the man in whose spirit this address is intended. Mann's words appear to me to be so very pertinent that I cannot refrain from citing them here. The writer, who late in his life overcame the bourgeois ironic view of death in order to attain to active enlightenment, proclaimed:

> To the inferior joy of all enemies of manly light, all priests of the dynamic orgasm, we have already reached the point of irrationality where the natural backlash is beginning to look viciously dangerous; and by now a backlash against the backlash appears necessary in order to frighten the chthonian rabble that has gotten too much grist for its mill back into the obscurity to which matriarchal right entitles it.

It is now crucial that the Enlightenment not permit itself to be intimidated, either by the traditional reproach—whose historical patina by no means renders it respectable—that it is "shallow," or by the modishly gesticulating, arrogant, but wholly unsound argument that it is "outdated." Analytic ratio does not become obsolete, unless by its own doing—whereby, to be sure, it invariably reconsolidates at the same time. Truth is certainly a difficult epistemological problem. In daily practice we are able to differentiate it from untruth. We need no philosophy of law in order to demand justice. Anyone who has ever lived in unfreedom knows what freedom is. Whoever was a victim of oppression can easily confirm from experience that equality is no myth. Reality is always more clever than the philosophy that impotently wishes to reflect it. That is why enlightenment is no seamless doctrinary construct but rather the constant illuminating dialogue that we are obliged to conduct with ourselves and with others. The light of the classical Enlightenment was no optical illusion, no hallucination. Where it threatens to disappear, humane consciousness becomes clouded. Whoever repudiates the Enlightenment is renouncing the education of the human race.

NOTES

After Five Thousand Newspaper Articles

1. *Jenseits von Schuld und Sühne* was published in the United States as *At the Mind's Limits: Contemplations by a Survivor on Auschwitz and Its Realities*, trans. Sidney Rosenfeld and Stella P. Rosenfeld (Bloomington: Indiana University Press, 1980).

In the Waiting Room of Death

1. Klabund was the pseudonym of the German writer, dramatist, and poet Alfred Henschke (1890–1928). The German lines read as follows: "Am Sonntag fällt ein kleines Wort im Dom / Am Montag rollt es wachsend durch die Gasse / Am Dienstag spricht man schon vom Rassenhasse / Am Mittwoch rauscht und raschelt es: Pogrom!"

Antisemitism on the Left

1. The "Red Orchestra" was an intelligence network during World War II that provided information about German military events to the Soviet Union.

Wasted Words

1. Hans Filbinger, the governor of the southwest German state of Baden-Württemberg, was forced to resign in 1978 when it was revealed that as a navy judge during the Third Reich he had zealously sentenced at least four German servicemen to death.

2. Possibly, this is an autobiographical allusion. In 1975 the prosecutor's office in Cologne initiated an investigation because of a—sensitive and misunderstood—statement Améry had made during a television round-table discussion in regard to the hunger strike of the imprisoned Baader-Meinhof terrorist group. The matter was soon dropped.

3. Victor Klemperer's revealing study of the language of Nazism was first published in 1947 under the title *LTI: Notizbuch eines Philologen* (Lingua Tertii Imperii: A philologist's notebook).

Nietzsche the Contemporary

1. *The Wisdom of Life* (1890) is the title of volume one of the English translation of Schopenhauer's *Aphorismen zur Lebensweisheit* (1886). The second volume is entitled *Counsels and Maxims* (1890).

2. The *Lebensborn* ("Well of Life") maternity homes were institutions of the SS founded by Himmler for the purpose of breeding racially superior children for the Third Reich.

The Limits of Perspicacity

1. Améry's reference is to Wittgenstein's *Das blaue Buch. Eine philosophische Betrachtung* (Frankfurt: Suhrkamp Verlag, 1970). This is a partial German version

done by Wittgenstein in 1936 of his *The Brown Book*. It later became Part One of *Philosophische Untersuchungen* (1954; *Philosophical Investigations*).

2. Wittgenstein's *Vermischte Bemerkungen* were first published in 1977 by Suhrkamp Verlag in Frankfurt. The English translation, edited by G. H. von Wright, was published in a bilingual edition under the title *Culture and Values* (Chicago: University of Chicago Press, 1980).

3. See note 1 under "Nietzsche the Contemporary."

Enlightenment as Philosophia Perennis

1. This is an allusion to the book *Der Untergang der Erde am Geist* (1924), by the philosopher Theodor Lessing (1877–1933). Lessing, the author of *Der jüdische Selbsthass* (1930; Jewish self-hate), was murdered by the Nazis in Czechoslovakia.

2. Améry's novel *Lefeu oder Der Abbruch* (Lefeu or the demolition) was published by Ernst Klett Verlag (Stuttgart) in 1974.